Church Curious

Church Curious

101 Interesting Facts About People,
Places and Things You Won't Learn on Sunday

Matthew C. Sidell

For Liz, Kody and Wren

Special thanks to the following persons or organizations who provided photographs or information that appear in this book: Seattle Pacific University, St. George's Episcopal Church of Fredericksburg, Arlington Temple United Methodist Church, Ann Minniear, YMCA Camp Greenville, Scott Riddle, St. Paul's Episcopal Church of Nantucket, Martin McKerrow, Father Max Wolf, The Church of Eight Wheels, Kelly Barclay, and Professor Mahmoud Manzalaoui.

Table of Contents

Introduction

I have always been drawn to the unique and the surprising that so often await just under the surface to be discovered. There are trivia books and lists covering a range of topics, but none so far as I am aware that focus specifically on Christianity and the church. So, I decided to write this little book to share some of my favorite discoveries. Each entry is short, no more than a few hundred words, and each is designed to edutain (educate and entertain).

During seminary, I spent a significant amount of time discovering all manner of interesting things. Some were quite surprising, such as the daily ration of alcohol for medieval monks (up to 2 gallons if you're wondering). Some are tragic, like the preferred method for executing early Anabaptists by drowning. Sometimes I found passing reference to things that proved impossible to confirm. For instance, Pietists invented raising your hand before speaking.

Quite often, the things that I learned led to wonder, joy and worship of an infinitely creative God who works in the lives of people in endlessly unique ways. Many of the things in this book were first discovered during those formative years studying under a green roof in Vancouver. Still more have come as things often do, while wandering from place to place or page to page. Whether you are a lover of trivia, a follower of Jesus, or both, I hope that this book will remind you of a few things that you knew, entertain you with new curiosities, and inspire you to seek an infinitely interesting God.

A Fine Puritan Name

Old Puritan names can be beautiful: Felicity, Hope, Prudence. But some from the late 16th and early 17th century can be quite bizarre. Parents often chose to give the child a name to serve as a reminder of some biblical truth or one that suggested an action for the child to take. A few more eccentric examples include: Helpless, Humiliation, Dust, Silence, Kill-Sin, Fight-the-Good-Fight-of-Faith, Abuse-Not, Fly-Fornication (female), and a member of British Parliament named Praise-God Barebone who had two sons named Jesus-Christ-Came-Into-The-World-To-Save and Unless-Christ-Had-Died-For-Thee-Thou-Hadst-Been-Damned. The latter, who would become a celebrated economist, more often went by the name Nicholas Barbon.

Praise-God Barebone. *Public Domain.*

The Oldest New Testament

The oldest known copy of any portion of the New Testament is a small fragment of papyrus from the Gospel of John known as P52. Measuring approximately 3.5in x 2.5in, it contains portions of John 18:31-33 and on the reverse side 18:37-38. With this information scholars have concluded that this fragment came from a bound copy of the gospel that was about 130 pages with each page approximately 8 inches x 8 inches.

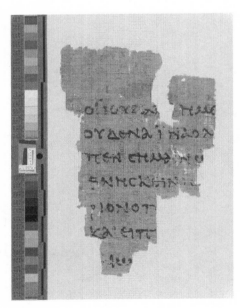

The fact that a sacred text from this era was written in a book and not a scroll continues to be the subject of significant scholarly interest. Books were generally used for trivial information like supply lists, but it appears that several early Christian texts were copied as books. The general consensus is that this copy was produced some time around 125-150AD. It is on permanent display in the Rylands Library at the University of Manchester.

P52 Recto or right side. *Rylands Imaging [CC BY-SA 4.0 (https://creativecommons.org/licenses/by-sa/4.0)]*

The Oldest Old Testament

The oldest known copy of any portion of the Old Testament is a pair of tiny silver scrolls that date to the 6th century BC. These predate the next oldest biblical texts, the Dead Sea Scrolls, by over four centuries. The scrolls which were probably worn as amulets include several lines of scripture, most notably the priestly benediction from Numbers 6:24-26. "The LORD bless you and keep you; the LORD make his face shine upon you and be

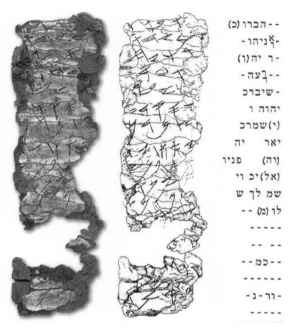

הברו (כ) - -
-אָניהו -
- ר יה(ו)
- בָעה - -
- שיברכ
יהוה ו
(י)שמרכ
יאר יה
(וה) פניו
(אל)יכ וי
שמ לך ש
לו (מ) - -
- - - - -
- - - -
- - כמ - -
- - - - - -
- ור - נ -
- - - - -

Larger of the two silver scrolls containing the priestly blessing. *Image Courtesy of Tamar Hayardeni.*

gracious to you; the LORD turn his face toward you and give you peace." The larger scroll when unrolled measures approximately 1.0 x 3.5 inches, while the smaller scroll is 0.5 x 1.5 inches. They were discovered in Jerusalem in 1979. Archaeologists and museum experts spent years deciding how to carefully unroll and read the scrolls. They are now a part of the collection held by the Israel Museum in Jerusalem.

Monastery. Meteora Monastery

The Meteora Monasteries in Greece were built on the tops of enormous natural rock pillars (as high as 1300ft) in the 14th century. They are truly a wonder to see perched so precariously. Originally, the only access was by long ropes or ladders that were replaced "when the Lord let them break". Six of the original twenty-four are occupied by monks or nuns today and are collectively considered a UNESCO world heritage site. One of the monasteries, Holy Trinity, appeared as the fictional abandoned St. Cyril's Monastery in the 1981 James Bond film *For Your Eyes Only*. The monks disapproved of the filming and after losing a legal battle went about sabotaging the film by hanging their laundry out in the supposedly "abandoned" monastery.

Holy   Trinity   Monastery.   *Dido3   [CC   BY-SA   3.0*
(http://creativecommons.org/licenses/by-sa/3.0/)]

The Original Barefoot Shoes

Monk-strap shoes are a popular semi-formal dress shoe named after the footwear worn by "barefoot" monks while doing manual labor. Discalced or barefoot monks date back to St. Francis c.1209AD who chose to go barefoot as part of a return to more rigorous practices of early monasticism. Over time some discalced monks began wearing open toed sandals which in turn were replaced by cap-toed sandals when working. These shoes gave inspiration to what eventually became the modern monk-strap.

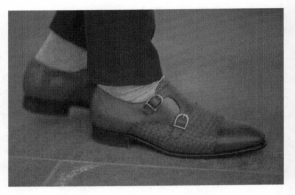

A modern monk-strap dress shoe. *Taftclothing [CC BY-SA 4.0 (https://creativecommons.org/licenses/by-sa/4.0)]*

Officially Licensed Monk Beer

Trappist Beer is named after a French Cistercian monastery named La Trappe Abbey which was the site of a reform movement in 1664 which sought to follow a more strict adherence to the Rule of St. Benedict. Officially called the Order of Cistercians of the Strict Observance, they became known as Trappists as other monasteries joined their movement and took on the name of the founding monastery. Today there are 168 Trappist monasteries or convents in the world. Only thirteen brew official Trappist beer, including Saint Sixtus Abbey which brews Westvleteren 12 which is widely considered one of the best beers in the world. In addition to their famous beer, Trappist-made products include cheese, jam, chocolate, cleaning products and baked goods. And one monastery in Hokkaido, Japan is famous for its butter cookies.

Beers from eleven of the thirteen Trappist Monasteries. Philip Rowlands [CC BY-SA 4.0 (https://creativecommons.org/licenses/by-sa/4.0)]

A Unique Color

The color chartreuse is named after the greenish yellow liqueur originally called the "Elixir of Long Life" produced by Carthusian monks since 1737. The drink which is mix of distilled alcohol and 130 herbs is based on a recipe given to the monks in 1605. The name actually comes from the name of the monastery, Grande Chartreuse, which is the original monastery of the Carthusian order (established 1084) and the subject of a 2005 documentary *Into Great Silence*. Only two monks know the precise combination of herbs for the liqueur. Today the monastery produces several liqueurs including the original elixir which is 138 proof (69% alcohol) and costs approximately $20 for a 3.5oz bottle.

Bottle of Chartreuse. *Zephyris* *[CC BY-SA 3.0* *(https://creativecommons.org/licenses/b* *y-sa/3.0)]*

Grande Chartreuse. *Floriel [CC BY-SA 3.0 (http://creativecommons.org/licenses/by-sa/3.0/)]*

A Hat Fit for a Duns

The dunce cap is named after one of the most influential medieval theologians, John Duns Scotus (1266-1308). John's name comes from the place of his birth, in the town of Duns in Berwickshire, Scotland. Scotus's ideas while important were often mind-numbingly difficult to follow. He is most famous for his defense of the immaculate conception, the idea that Mary was conceived without sin. Philosophers who followed Scotus were called Scotists or Dunsmen or sometimes simply Duns (pronounced "dunce"). After about 200 years, his ideas began to fall out of fashion. To be a "dunce" came to mean someone hopelessly behind the times intellectually. As for the eponymous headwear, Scotus and his followers were known to wear a soft cone shaped hat similar to those depicted on the Magi in early Christian art. The cap was thought to be a funnel for the mind and a symbol of learning. The first written use of the word dunce cap is a passing reference from Dickens' *Old Curiosity Shop*, first published in 1840.

John Duns Scotus. *Public Domain.*

10

Jesus the Stone Mason?

Joseph (right) depicted as a carpenter in Merone Altarpiece by Robert Campin c.1427. *Public Domain.*

Jesus is often described as a carpenter, but there are only two biblical references to his occupation, Mark 6:3 and Matthew 13:55. In both cases the word used is *tekton* which could mean carpenter but is more generally a craftsman or builder. Because of the relative scarcity of wood in the region and how often Jesus referenced stone masonry, it is sometimes thought that Jesus was more likely a stone mason or builder. Whatever his specific occupation, Jesus probably worked in the Galilean capital city of Sepphoris which was only about an hour's walk from Nazareth and was experiencing significant growth at the time. Interestingly, Sepphoris is thought to be the home town of Jesus' mother Mary though the city is not mentioned in the bible. The earliest specific reference to Jesus as a carpenter is from Justin Martyr (c. 160AD) who mentions that Jesus made ploughs and yokes. As for why most English bibles translate *tekton* as carpenter, you can thank William Tyndale. Following his 1526 translation which used "carpenter" nearly every other translation did the same.

A Picture of Jesus

Warner Sallman is the most famous artist you've never heard of. Sallman was a painter and illustrator whose work has been reproduced over 500 million times. His most famous work is a painting called the Head of Christ. In fact, I bet when you picture Jesus in your mind, he probably looks a lot like the Sallman painting. Shoulder length brown wavy hair, a beard, a slightly pale face with an intense but serene gaze looking ever so slightly upward. The original picture was a charcoal sketch done in 1924 for his denomination's magazine, but the widely reproduced version was commissioned in 1940 for North Park Theological Seminary. It was intended to be a masculine portrayal of Jesus and was handed out to soldiers by the USO during WWII. Duke University professor David Morgan, who has written several books on Sallman thinks that the Cold War was when Sallman's work became the quintessential American Jesus unifying the church denominations against communism. Today, Sallman's work is not especially admired and its proliferation is seen as promoting an incorrect picture of Jesus. Incidentally, Sallman's brother-in-law Haddon Sundblom was the man responsible for the quintessential Santa Clause. Sundblom painted the image for Coca Cola in 1931.

Fourteenthers

Some holidays are celebrated on a specific day of the week, like Thanksgiving. Others are celebrated on a specific date of the year, like Christmas. You might be surprised to know that there was a major controversy in the early church about whether to celebrate Easter on a day (Sunday) or on specific date on the Jewish lunar calendar (14th of Nisan, the beginning of Passover). Predominately in Jerusalem and Asia Minor, those that advocated for the 14th of Nisan were called Quartodecimani, Latin for "fourteenthers". They would gather after sundown, which marks the beginning of a new day, to celebrate the Lord's Supper as a part of Jewish Passover. As Christianity became more gentile and less connected to Jewish practice, churches began celebrating on the Sunday following the 14th of Nisan out of a desire to acknowledge Sunday as the day of the resurrection.

What a Name

There is a famous puritan pastor named Richard Baxter (1615-1691) with an unforgettable nickname. Baxter was a pastor in the English town of Kidderminster for seventeen years during which time he converted nearly all of the 2000 people in the town. He left Kidderminster for five years to serve as a chaplain during the English civil war. These significant periods of ministry led him to write two of his

Portrait of Richard Baxter by Robert White. *Public Domain.*

most famous works: *The Reformed Pastor* and *The Saints Everlasting Rest*. These two books are a small part of his complete writings. Baxter was a prolific writer with over 200 published works. His longest book *Christian Directory* contains over a million words. As you may have guessed, his nickname comes from his writing prowess. He was known as Scribbling Dick.

A Man Named Useful

One of the briefest books in the Bible is the letter to Philemon. It concerns a run-away slave named Onesimus who upon meeting Paul is converted to Christianity and subsequently sent back to his master to be received as a brother. Onesimus, which means "useful", was an extremely common name for a slave. Part of Paul's argument is that Onesimus was formerly useless to his master, but has now because of Christ finally lived up to his name. This is one of only two personal letters (3 John is the other) in the New Testament. Its contents are very narrowly focused on Paul's request for Onesimus. Yet it is included in the very earliest canonical lists. So why was it included in scripture? One possible reason is that a certain bishop of Ephesus was the first to gather all of Paul's letters together and publish them. That bishop's name was Onesimus.

Tile Mosaic of Onesimus. *Public Domain.*

A Pastor for Pastors

John Chrysostom (c.349-407) is one of the most significant early church fathers on par with Augustine and Irenaeus. Many of his ideas and pastoral practices have become commonplace in a church today, although there are a few that were a bit eccentric. For example, as a monk he spent two years standing on his feet in an attempt to be ever watchful for the Lord. After a few years as a monk, he became the

John Chrysostom. *Public Domain.*

leader of the church in Constantinople where he was known as a great preacher. He preached verse by verse, book by book. He used vivid illustrations and pneumonic devices in his preaching and it was not uncommon for people to become overwhelmed at his preaching. Rousing applause and weeping were both common occurrences at his sermons. His most influential work is a book written for pastors called *On the Priesthood* in which he advocates for a high calling for clergy and, in a way that rings true today, a plea for pastors to have at least one deep friendship.

Eight Cold Churches

Antarctica has a population of only a few thousand people, but it is home to eight churches. Most are Catholic or Orthodox and are built on a particular host country's research base. Chapel of St. Francis of Assisi is on an

Trinity Church at Bellinghausen, Antarctica. *Photo by James L. Boka [CC BY-SA 3.0 (https://creativecommons.org/licenses/by-sa/3.0)]*

Argentinian base and was the site of the first Antarctic wedding. Chapel of the Blessed Virgin of Lujan is on another Argentinian research base. St. Mary Queen of Peace Chapel is on a Chilean research station. Chapel of the Snows is the only nondenominational church and is on a United States research base. St. Ivan Rilski Chapel is part of the Bulgarian base on Livingston Island. St. Volodymyr Chapel is the smallest chapel, built in 2011 on the Ukrainian base. The beautiful Trinity Church is a traditional Russian orthodox church manned year-round by two priests. Rounding out the list is the most eccentric. Chapel of Our Lady of the Snows is also an Argentinian church, and it is carved out of an ice cave. It is the southernmost place of worship in the world.

The Prince of Preachers

Charles Spurgeon (1834-1892) was the most famous preacher of the 19th century. At just 19 he was invited to be the pastor of the dwindling congregation at New Park Street Chapel where he remained for the next 38 years. By the age of 22, he was preaching to a congregation of 10,000 on a Sunday. Spurgeon was a voracious reader from a young age and is said to have had a photographic memory. As an adult he read six books a week and often worked 18 hours per day. He would carry a notebook with him to write down sermon ideas throughout the week, but he did most of his prep work with his wife on Saturday night. Copies of Spurgeon's sermons were sold for a penny per week. The proceeds helped to fund the preachers college that he founded at age 20. In the evenings he would teach 100-200 students (many from the very poorest of

London) the art of preaching. By the time of his death Spurgeon had published more than 3500 sermons as well as over 140 other books. If that weren't enough, he also was the founder of some 66 different associations on issues like orphan care and church planting.

Spurgeon preaching at the Crystal Palace.
Public Domain.

A Pietist's Personal Space

Francke as a child. *Public Domain.*

August Hermann Francke (1663-1727) was one of the leaders of a movement within German Lutheranism called Pietism. Francke's was especially noteworthy for his contribution in educating children. What is less well known is that as a child Francke was a pioneer in a novel practice that is taken for granted today. At the time, it was common for families to share one living and sleeping space. But Francke around age 11 requested and was given a private room so that he could retreat to so that he might pray. Most homes today are built with several smaller bedrooms but the practice has its roots in the desire for individual places of solitude to be with God.

Ethiopian Rock Churches

In Ethiopia, there are eleven monolithic churches carved out of rock at a site known as Lalibela. Around the world, there are other amazing monolithic structures carved from rock such as the famous city of Petra. What makes Lalibela unique is that many of these churches were carved top-down from ground level, some as deep as 45 meters. Bet Giyorgis (Church of St. George) with its intricate cross shape is the most famous and most well preserved. These churches are thought to have been carved around the 12th century by King Lalibela and his men, who according to legend built everything with the assistance of angels.

(above) Bet Giyorgis from above. *Julien Demade* [CC BY-SA 3.0 *(https://creativecommons.org/licenses/by-sa/3.0)]*

(below) Bet Giyorgis at ground level. *Giustino* [CC BY 2.0 *(https://creativecommons.org/licenses/by/2.0)]*

Lalibela is a UNESCO World Heritage site and despite its remote location, it is a major destination for tourists and pilgrims alike. Worship services are still held on Sundays and can have hundreds of Ethiopian Orthodox faithful.

Cult-like Cutlery

Oneida, one of the world's largest makers of tableware and cutlery was begun as a way of financially supporting an extremely fringe group of supposed Christians who founded a commune in 1848 in Oneida, New York. Among the Oneida Community's beliefs was the idea that Jesus' second coming had already occurred and that individuals could live a sin free life. They held all property in common including the responsibility to raise children which led to a practice they called complex marriage, where members were free to be with anyone else who consented. Parents were forbidden to bond with children who were raised in a separate wing of the commune. To support their community, they engaged in a variety of businesses including production of animal traps, leather bags, garden furniture, silk, hats, and canning. Their community grew to about 300 members but their controversial beliefs led to tensions inside and outside of the community. As the community collapsed, the remaining 70 members reorganized as a joint-stock corporation in 1881. The tableware business didn't begin until 1899 after many of their earlier businesses became unprofitable.

Stereoscope of front Lawn of Oneida Mansion. *New York Public Library [Public domain]*

21

Non-alcoholic Communion Wine

Thomas Bramwell Welch. *Public Domain.*

Thomas Bramwell Welch (1825-1903) was a dentist, a Methodist and a Prohibitionist. He was also an active supporter of the Underground Railroad. In 1865, Welch moved to Vineland, New Jersey, a newly built town designed to be an alcohol-free community that happened to be well suited to growing grapes. In 1869, Welch invented a way to pasteurize grape juice so that it wouldn't become alcoholic. He convinced a number of churches to use "Dr. Welch's Unfermented Wine" during communion. Thomas and his son Charles, also a dentist, had a business selling dental supplies and occasionally sold their grape juice on the side. As the temperance movement grew, the Welch's Grape Juice Company was formed in 1893 to meet the demand for unfermented wine.

A Sing-Song Debate

In the third century there was a major debate in the church about whether Jesus was really God or not. On one side of the debate was Athanasius, Bishop of Alexandria who argued that Jesus was fully God because he was begotten (not made) by the Father. Therefore, Father and Son share the same substance and are coequals. On the other side was a priest named Arius who argued that Jesus was less than God because he was created by the Father. The debate lasted over 50 years and got pretty heated. One particularly successful method of persuasion that Arius used was songs

Athanasius. *Public Domain.*

(left) Arius. *Public Domain*

and chants. His followers would go around singing, "There was a time when he was not" in order to convince everyone that Jesus was a creature made by God. At many points it looked as if Arius had won. Athanasius was exiled on five different occasions. The debate

appeared to be settled when the Council of Nicea (325 AD) overwhelmingly agreed with Athanasius, but political and religious power struggles kept the argument alive until 381 AD when the Nicene Creed was reaffirmed at the Second Ecumenical Council. To emphasize that the debate was truly over, the council added a statement at the end of the creed that those who say "there was a time when he was not" are condemned by the church.

Uncials, Majuscules and Minuscules

IMAGINETRYINGTOREADEVERYTHINGLIKETHISSENTENC
EWITHOUTPUNCTUATIONORLOWERCASELETTERSORSPACE
SBETWEENWORDS. This is actually what some of the earliest
copies of the Bible look like. This script is called uncial or majuscule
and was the standard for formal Greek writing until around the 9th
century AD when lower case letters based on the less formal cursive
Greek alphabet began to appear. Gradually, spacing between words
and punctuation marks came
into practice as well. These
later texts are called
minuscules. The term
majuscule means "of a fair
size" while minuscule means
"rather small". Uncial means
about an inch high and comes
from St. Jerome's preface to the
book of Job in his Latin
translation of the Bible.
Understanding the distinct
writing styles and the time
periods in which they were
used help experts to date even
very small fragments of ancient
texts. People who study the
gradual changes in writing are
called paleographers.

Codex Alexandrinus, a majuscule.
British Library. Public domain.

24

Pointy Headwear

Cone shaped head wear has a long history in the church. It is thought that they earliest of these dates back to the Phrygian cap, a soft cone shaped hat from around the 4th century which was commonly depicted on the magi in early Christian art. Bishops from about the 12th century have worn a mitre in formal settings, a conical hat similar to the eponymous chess piece. The Gugel (German) or Chaperon (French) or Capuccio (Italian) was a popular piece of conical headwear taking on many forms in medieval Europe. It was a hooded cape worn in a variety of styles, often with the conical cape draped down the back by both men and women. Modern academic robes are a holdover of this fashion. For centuries monks have worn hooded robes, but it is the brown-robed Capuchin monks for whom the cappuccino is named because of the similar color of the frothy espresso to their robes.

Phrygian Cap from 2nd Century.
Cabinet des Médailles. Public domain.

(above left) Illustration of a chaperon from the 13th century Morgan Bible. *Public Domain.*

25

Unique Churches

There are so many churches that are unique that it's hard to keep track of them all. There is a drive-in theater styled church in Daytona Beach, Florida. Lalibella is a collection of Ethiopian churches carved underground out of the rock. In Allouville-Bellefosse, France there is a thousand-year-old oak tree that has not just one, but two chapels built inside its hollow trunk. In 2011 a New Zealand man began an impressive task to build a living church out of trees that can seat 100 people. In the country of Georgia, there is a small church built on the

Katshiki Pillar. *Arkaitz1974 [CC BY-SA 4.0 (https://creativecommons.org/licenses/by-sa/4.0)]*

top of a 120ft Limestone column known as the Katskhi Pillar. At a YMCA camp there is an open-air chapel known as Pretty Place with stunning views of the Blue Ridge Mountains. St. Simon the Tanner Church, one of the largest churches in Egypt, is built in a cave and serves a Coptic congregation of trash pickers.

Pretty Place at YMCA Camp Greenville. *Image Courtesy of Scott Riddle.*

(below) Saint Simon Monastery. *Ehab ahmed mohammed [CC BY-SA 4.0 (https://creativecommons.org/licenses/by-sa/4.0)]*

Throw 'em out the Window

Defenestration is one of the more interesting albeit grim terms in church history. It refers to the act of tossing someone out of a window, typically to their death. While there are many occurrences of defenestration, it is most well-known because of the two separate occurrences in 1419 and 1618 that are collectively known as the Defenestration of Prague. The Czech Kingdom was grappling with political, social and economic tensions that were further complicated by a growing divide within the church. The first defenestration occurred because of mounting tensions between the Catholics and the Hussites, a group who wanted to reform the church by force if necessary. The 1419 defenestration marked the beginning of the Hussite War. The 1618 defenestration happened after Catholic officials in Bohemia were responsible for closing protestant churches in the city. The three officials survived the 70 foot fall with Catholics claiming angels caught them and protestants later claiming they fell into a pile of dung. This event precipitated the Thirty Years War.

Defenestration of Prague. Engraving by Matthäus Merian. *Public domain.*

Three Mythical Creatures

In Jewish mythology there are 3 great creatures that dominated separate parts of the world. One to rule the sea. One to rule the land. One to rule the sky. Two of these creatures are mentioned in the book of Job.

Image of Leviathan, Behemoth and Ziz from 13th century Ambrosiana Bible. *Public domain.*

Leviathan is the great sea creature mentioned in Job 41. Behemoth is the great monster of the land mentioned in Job 40. But what about the sky? This belongs to the great winged creature called Ziz, which is said to have wings wide enough to blot out the sun. Jewish mythology isn't alone in describing a birdlike great beast. Several versions of a winged creature appear in other ancient mythological texts such as the Simurgh of Persia or the Phoenix of Greek mythology. Though no explicit biblical reference exists, there is a vaguely passing reference that is usually lost when translating from Hebrew in Psalm 50:11. While Leviathan and Behemoth get most of the attention, not to mention the cooler names, all three creatures are attested in extrabiblical writings as being under the control and dominion of God.

The First Suburb

William Wilberforce and the Clapham Sect are most famous for their nearly twenty-year effort to abolish the slave trade. But they also happen to have pioneered a new type of community, the suburb. Up to the 18th century, the periphery of a city was worst place to live with everyone aspiring to live in the city center. This began to change when Wilberforce moved to Clapham in 1792. Clapham became a place uniquely suited for Wilberforce and other prominent evangelicals to practice engagement and withdrawal. It was an idyllic refuge from the city and gave them a safe place to raise and educate children and to practice neighborliness. It is hard to imagine, but these were entirely novel ideas at the time. It was the model of Clapham that spread from London throughout England to Australia, America and beyond. In less than a century, the suburb became the predominate place where people lived.

Clapham Commons, 1841. *Public Domain.*

Hobbies for Pastors

Many pastors have a hobby that serves as a creative outlet. Phillip Jakob Spener (1631-1705) was an influential German Pietist pastor who is often credited with establishing small group ministry. He also happened to be an expert in Heraldry, which is the study and design of coats of arms. Eugene Peterson has written several books of poetry. There is a Benedictine monk known as Brother Adam (1898-1996) who was a world-famous beekeeper. John Stott loved birdwatching so much that he wrote a book entitled, *The Birds Our Teachers* about it. Francis Chan is an avid surfer, which isn't technically a creative outlet, but Chan did make a short film about surfing. John Wesley had a hobby of practicing and cataloguing medical remedies, particularly electric shock therapy. The very first car in America was invented by a minister in Wisconsin in 1873.

Brother Adam with his beehives. *HW59 [CC BY-SA 4.0 (https://creativecommons.org/licenses/by-sa/4.0)]*

Nicknames

Church history is littered with amusing nicknames. Saint Athanasius (296-373AD) was a short Egyptian bishop nicknamed the Black Dwarf by his enemies. Thomas Aquinas (1225-1274AD) was called the Dumb Ox by his classmates because of his quiet demeanor and unfortunate bad looks. Antony of Padua (1195-1231AD) was known as the Hammer of Heretics. Hilary of Poitiers (310-367AD) was called the Hammer of Arians. Martin Luther (1483-1546) was called the Philosopher. John Newton the slave trader turned pastor who penned "Amazing Grace" was known as the Old Blasphemer. There is an early dessert monk called Paul the Simple. St. Theresa of Lisieux (1873-1897) was known as the Little Flower of Jesus. My personal favorite is Symeon of Emesa (d. 570AD) who was known as the Holy Fool. Symeon feigned insanity in order that his good deeds would be done in secret. His preferred charade was extinguishing the lights and throwing food at people.

The Dumb Ox, Thomas Aquinas by Carlo Crivelli. *Public domain.*

Alcohol Churches

Presented without comment, here are a few churches with alcohol themed names. Bourbon Bible Church is one of three churches located in Bourbon, Indiana. Similarly, in both Ohio and Illinois there are counties named Champaign (pronounced like the bubbly drink) home to many eponymous churches. There is a Martini Lutheran Church in Baltimore, MD which would fit well with St. James-Bond Church in Toronto. Years before writing his spy stories Ian Fleming visited a friend who lived near the church. Fans speculate this may have been where he got the name. There are many coastal places of worship named Port Church. Drunk Church is a recovery-based church in Knoxville, TN. Atlanta has a Bar Church, which as the name suggests meets for "liquid liturgies" in a local bar. In Johannesburg, South Africa there is a men's only church that celebrates drinking, and actively encourages people to drink during the service. The name, Gabola Church, comes from the Tswana word for "drinking". Unsurprisingly, the founder of Gabola Church, Bishop Tsietsi Makita died in 2018 from alcohol abuse.

Magic Words

The origins of the magic words "Hocus Pocus" are a bit difficult to ascertain, but there is one plausible theory that dates back to the 1600s. The words come from a phrase that was seen to have the power to transform objects. During mass at a Catholic church there is a moment when the priest prepares the Eucharist. The Catholic church believes in transubstantiation, that the bread and wine actually become the body and blood of Jesus. By repeating the words Christ said at the Last Supper, the priest's words would serve to consecrate the bread and wine thereby turning them into the body and blood of Christ. These words, spoken in Latin, are "hoc est enim corpus meum". Over time these words were corrupted when they were misheard or misspoken into the magic words we know today, hocus pocus.

Old Testament by Another Name

Jews in Jesus' day didn't refer to the 39 books of Genesis through Malachi as the Old Testament. These books were instead grouped into three categories: Torah (Law), Nevi'im (Prophets) and Ketuvim (Writings). They were thus referred to by the acronym Tanakh. This is the way that Jesus refers to the scriptures in Luke 24:44. Torah includes the first five books of scripture. Nevi'im includes historical books like Joshua as well books named after prophets such as Jeremiah and Obadiah. Ketuvim is the most difficult to categorize since it includes poetic, historical and prophetic books. As is often

the case, there is a bit of controversy with naming the Hebrew scriptures. Some scholars believe that there were originally only two categories: Law and Prophets. They argue that distinguishing between Prophets and Writings was a later concept dating to the 4th century AD. Lending a bit of credence to their claim is the fact that most of the time, people in the New Testament use the two-fold term Law and Prophets as in Matthew 5:17. In any case, Tanakh is a well attested way to refer to the Hebrew scriptures.

A parchment of Torah. *Davidbena*
[CC BY-SA 4.0
(https://creativecommons.org/licenses/by-sa/4.0)]

Stone Bread

During the temptation of Jesus, Satan tells him to turn a stone into bread (Matthew 4:3 and Luke 4:3). In the desert region where Jesus' temptation took place there are stones known by geologists as septaria. The name comes from the Latin word for "partition" referring to the many cracks along the surface of the stone. These

Septaria that looks a bit like petrified bread.
Matt (kwinkunks on Flickr)
https://www.flickr.com/people/kwinkunks/ [CC BY 2.0
(https://creativecommons.org/licenses/by/2.0)]

stones were formed as a certain type of mud clumped and very slowly turned to stone. Eventually the stones cracked making way for other minerals to enter giving the stones their distinctive looks. Septaria can be many shapes and sizes, but some bear a striking resemblance to a loaf of bread. In fact, there is evidence that these stones were thought to be petrified food. Similar to the effect of seeing a mirage, the presence of petrified food would have made a starving man hunger more.

Pew Rents

Collecting a weekly offering during worship services is a relatively recent practice begun in the mid 19th century as part of what was ironically called the free church movement. At the time, most protestant churches were financed by pew rents, annual fees paid to lease the exclusive use of an enclosed family seat in the sanctuary. By law only a small number or seats, usually simple benches in the worst parts of the church, were required to be rent free. Gradually, it became clear that this practice was excluding the most vulnerable from church. Many opposed the practice but were fearful of churches losing their primary source of income. The London Free and Open Church Association was one of a handful of groups advocating for churches to adopt a new source of income, a weekly offering. While they were extremely successful in mostly abolishing the practice, pew-renting continued to exist in small numbers up until the 1950s when it was almost entirely abandoned. The last holdout was a remote church that continued collecting pew rents up until 2008.

Seating Plan of St George's Church in 1849

| 4 Mrs. J. D. Taylor $350 | 3 J. B. Ficklen $450 | 2 Mrs. Coalter / Chs. Herndon $460 | 1 Rector | Desk | Pulpit | Desk | | 100 T. B. Barton $405 | 99 R. W. Carter $380 | 98 J. T. Lamay $355 | 97 Mrs. Hunter $310 |

Pews Sold April 23d, 1849 — Table — Chancel — Church partially burnt. July 1854

○ Communion Rail ○

Pew	Left name	Right name	Pew
5	J. Coakely $315	Capt Hamilton $385	72
6	M. H. Crump $295	Dr. J. B. Hall $395	70
7	A. Goodwin $295	M. Forbes $400	68
8	Mrs. J. R. Harrison $320	D. H. Gordon $405 C. Wistar Wallace	66
9	Thos. Pratt $310	Misses Fitzhugh $415	64
10	M. Slaughter $325	Dr. J. H. Wallace $400 A.W.W.	62
11	Mrs. V. Carmichael $245	W. K. Gordon $400 Dr. A. G. Doggett	60
12	Mrs. A. S. Hayes $275	H. Fitzhugh $385	58
13	Dr. B. S. Herndon $290	T. F. Knox $370	56
14	Mrs. J. B. Gray $290	T. F. Knox $370	54
15	Dr. J. Cooke $280	Dr. J. G. Wallace $360	52
16	W. C. L. Rothrock $230 Robt. Hall	Dr. J. R. Taylor $340	50
17	F. J. Wiatt $255	Y. Smith $325 J. Z. Stansbury	48
18	W. R. Mason, Jr. $240	Y. Smith $325 Dr. W. M. Smith	46
19	J. W. Johnston $230	Dr. Carmichael $300	44
20	N. Fitzhugh $225	J. J. Berry $280	42
21	Jane H. Dickinson $225	R. D. Minor $255	40
22	Mrs. Ellis	Paul Clay $255	38
		$200 Buck	

Pew	Left name	Right name	Pew
73	R. C. L. Moncure $310	Dr. Wm. Browne $340	96
71	Miss Agnes Gray St. G. R. Fitzhugh $390	P. Goolrick $275	95
69	Mrs. Scott Dr. Wm. S. Scott $385	Geo. B. Scott $280	94
67	Mrs. F. Scott Mrs. Allen $385	Dr. H. Morson $295	93
65	J. F. Scott J. P. Corbin $400	A. K. Phillips $300	92
63	Hugh Scott B. S. Herndon $400	Benj. Temple $290 A. B. Botts	91
61	S. Phillips $370	W. S. Barton $245 A. B. Botts, Sr.	90
59	Jno. Hart $360	C. S. Scott $245	89
57	Miss Jane Hart E. M. Braxton $360	H. B. Hoomes $265	88
55	Jno. L. Chinn $355	Misses Pearson $265	87
53	Wm. Pollock $330	W. H. Cunningham $255	86
51	Capt. J. Rudd $325	J. J. Young $230	85
49	J. M. Whittemore $300	T. H. Botts $225	84
47	F. Slaughter $290	Duff Green $225	83
45	J. W. Lucas $300	Miss Goodwin $225	82
43	J. H. Roberts F. W. Johnston $270	Dr. Mason $225	81
41	M. A. Blankman $245	J. Galleher $225	80
39	Mrs. A. J. Fitzhugh $225	Jno. Minor $200	79
		Mrs. Smock	78

Where there is a lower name on a pew, it is generally that of a subsequent purchaser.

Seating chart with prices of pew rents. *Courtesy of St. George's Episcopal Church, Fredericksburg, Virginia.*

Gas Station Church

Arlington Temple United Methodist Church located just across the river from Washington, D.C. is a relatively nondescript church with one major exception. It is the only church in America built over top of a gas station. In the 1960s the area was quickly becoming more urbanized. William Ames, Sr., a local businessman planned to convert his lumberyard into a new hotel. To do so he also needed to relocate a gas station occupying part of the future hotel land. At the

Arlington Temple with gas prices in red visible and hotel in background. *Courtesy of Ann Minniear and Arlington Temple United Methodist Church.*

same time, Ames donated a portion of the north end of his property to build Arlington Temple. Together it was decided to relocate the gas station to the donated church property and build the church above the new gas station so that the church could earn revenue from leasing the ground level. It proved to be a savvy financial decision providing a steady stream of income to support the church's mission and expenses. Even though there is currently a Sunnoco station on site, Arlington Temple was known for years

Cemeteries and Graveyards

What is the difference between a cemetery and a graveyard? A cemetery is a place to bury the remains of the dead. A graveyard serves the same purpose, but is located within church grounds. For centuries, burials were the responsibility of the church and a proper Christian burial could only happen on church grounds. By the 19th century in Europe, attitudes toward graveyards began to change due to urbanization, overcrowding, and the spread of disease from decay. A solution was sought that would alleviate these problems. In 1804 Père Lachaise was the first major cemetery, built on the outskirts of Paris as a beautiful and well-designed burial site for people regardless of race or religion. Before the advent of public parks, it became a popular place for social outings. Gradually, as famous Parisians were buried there, it became a popular burial place for others as well. London followed in 1832 with the establishment of seven beautiful cemeteries of its own that are collectively known as the Magnificent Seven.

Engraving of Père Lachaise by Pierre Courvoisier, 1815.
Public domain.

Moses with Horns

There is a famous sculpture of Moses by Michelangelo that was commissioned in 1505 for the tomb of Pope Julius II. The nearly 8ft tall sculpture depicts a seated Moses holding the Ten Commandments with a long beard and flowing robes. It is beautiful but also peculiar for one very strange reason. Moses has horns. In the 4th century, Saint Jerome translated the bible into Latin, known as the Vulgate. When he got to Exodus 34:29 he is thought to have mistranslated the Hebrew word "keren" which can mean both "horn" and "ray of light" so that the text reads, "he did not know

that his face was horned from the conversation of the LORD." There is some debate as to whether Jerome made a mistake or if he meant to use horns as a symbolic representation of God's glory. Some other famous examples of a horned Moses include the stained glass window at Chartres Cathedral and a large statue known as "First Down Moses" on the campus of Notre Dame.

Moses sculpture by Michelangelo.
Jörg Bittner Unna [CC BY 3.0 (https://creativecommons.org/licenses/by/3.0)]

42

Not One Iota

An iota is the smallest Greek letter and often symbolically used to represent small things. This idea is seen in Matthew 5:18 when Jesus says, "For truly, I say to you, until heaven and earth pass away, not an iota, not a dot, will pass from the Law until all is accomplished." In modern speech, to say that you don't care about something one iota is to say you don't care even a little bit. But there was a time when an iota mattered a great deal.

In the 3rd century debate between Athanasius and Arius about whether Jesus was really God, an iota made all the difference. In order to better understand, you need to know a little Greek. *ousious* is the Greek word for essence, substance. The Greek word for same is *homo*, and the Greek word for similar is *homoi*. Athanasius argued that the Father and the Son shared the same substance, *homoousious*. Arius said that they only shared a similar substance, *homoiousious*. That one little iota caused a major debate in the church that lasted over 50 years.

This Town goes to Eleven

Solothurn is a lovely old town in Switzerland located between Bern to the south and Basel to the north. It is famous for its baroque architecture and beautiful old town. But it is perhaps best known for its affinity for the number eleven. It was the eleventh to join the Swiss Confederation, has eleven historic fountains, eleven chapels, eleven museums, eleven towers, and even an eleven hour clock. But the crown jewel of elevens is the Cathedral of St. Urus (completed in 1773). Outside there are three sets of eleven stairs flanked by two fountains each containing eleven spigots. The church has eleven doors. The belfry is 66m high and contains precisely 11 bells. Inside are 11 altars with one containing 11 kinds of marble. All eleven altars are only visible from one spot, marked by the eleventh flagstone in the cathedral floor. It is said to have taken eleven years to build.

(above) Eleven hour clock. Drzamich [CC BY-SA 3.0 (https://creativecommons.org/licenses/by-sa/3.0)]

(right) St. Urus Cathedral with fountains visible. *Userhelp.ch at de.wikipedia [CC BY-SA 3.0 de (https://creativecommons.org/licenses/by-sa/3.0/de/deed.en)]*

French Royal Tombs

The Basilica of Saint Denis is located in the northern suburbs of Paris. It is architecturally significant as the first truly gothic church with towering ceilings and amazing stained-glass windows, the most stunning of which are in the chancel. The church is built upon the burial site of Saint Denis, the first martyred bishop of Paris. A popular pilgrimage site because of the fame of Saint Denis, it became the preferred burial site for nearly every French monarch beginning with Dagobert I (603-639 AD) and ending with Louis XVIII (1755-1824 AD). During the French Revolution, many of the remains of the royals were desecrated, dumped in a mass grave and covered with lime to destroy the bodies. Eventually, the remains were recovered

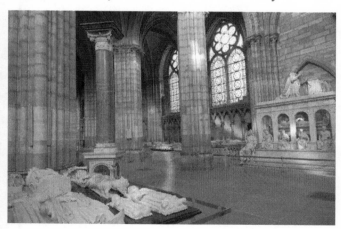

and most placed back in an ossuary in the church. Fortunately, most of the funerary statues and tombs were not destroyed and are in their original condition and locations for tourists to see today.

Interior of Basilica. *Guilhem Vellut from Paris, France [CC BY 2.0 (https://creativecommons.org/licenses/by/2.0)]*

3D Printed Armor

The Swiss Guard are protectors of the Pope and have been since 1506. With only a hundred soldiers, they are the world's smallest standing army. They are known for their striped blue, orange, yellow and red uniforms that have a distinctly Renaissance appearance. This is primarily a ceremonial role, although members of the guard do actually serve as plainclothes bodyguards for the pope as well. To be considered for the guard, one must be a single Catholic male between 19-30 years old with Swiss citizenship. While they are trained to use modern weapons, the traditional halberd

Swiss Guardman inspecting his helmet. *Willem van de Poll [CC0]*

and sword along with forged metal armor are carried while in ceremonial uniform. The metal helmets are an especially heavy, and in summer months, the hotest part of the attire. Much to the delight of the soldiers, in January of 2019 the Swiss Guard made headlines by deciding to replace the traditional forged metal helmets with 3D printed plastic helmets. Besides being lighter, they're also cheaper and easier to make. The metal helmets would take an expert blacksmith around 125 hours to make one, while a new 3D printed helmet can be completed in 14 hours.

Julian of Norwich

An anchorite (male) or anchoress (female) is a person who has deliberately chosen to live in permanent seclusion typically within a cell attached to a church. They take formal vows of stability and live a consecrated life, devoting themselves to prayer and communion with God. A typical cell had a window into the church to view the altar and receive the Eucharist and a window looking out into the world. While they chose seclusion, they were often keenly engaged with the broader world and had a reputation for wisdom. The most famous anchoress was an English woman known as Julian of

Norwich (1342-1416) who lived during a period of intense suffering. Within the church, heretics were being condemned. Outside the church people were dying of the Black Plague. She wrote of her experiences in a book *Revelations of Divine Love* which was the first book known to written by a woman in English. It has given wisdom and comfort to suffering people for centuries. The most enduring of her writing describes a vision in which Jesus said to her, "All shall be well. And All shall be well. Every manner of

Statue of Julian of Norwich by David Holgate adorning Norwich Cathedral. *Poliphilo [CC0]*

47

Birthday Bone Fire

John the Baptist was born about six months prior to Jesus according to the Gospel of Luke. That places his birthday around the time of the summer solstice. The solstice marks the point when the daylight grows shorter which was the perfect reminder of John's statement that John must decrease. From at least the 13th century, Christians have celebrated John's birth on the solstice with fire. Though the exact reason seems lost to history, one of the earliest accounts of this celebration specifically mentions the burning of bones called a bonfire. Over time, the name bonfire became more generally associated with a celebratory fire around which people gather. Though most countries have almost entirely forgotten the Christian origin of the solstice bonfires, several still celebrate the summer solstice by lighting huge bonfires. In fact, the world's largest bonfire, Slinningsbålet, happens in the coastal town of Alesund, Norway every June. The world record for tallest bonfire of 47.4 meters was set here in 2016.

Midsummer Eve Bonfire. *Peder Severin Krøyer [Public domain]*

Great Saint Bernard Hospice

In 1046 a monk named Bernard of Menthon was tasked with caring for the poor and any travelers passing through the city of Aosta, situated in a valley near the Italian border with Switzerland. Many of the travelers were pilgrims on their way to Rome and had to use a path through the Alps that would often have many feet of snow. Bernard decided to build a hostel at the highest point along the path as a place of refuge for travelers. Originally named for Saint Nicholas, patron saint of travelers, it was eventually renamed after it founder. The Great Saint Bernard Hospice as it is now known has been continuously open to guests for nearly a thousand years. The famed dogs were gifted to the monks in the 1670s and are said to have rescued nearly 2000 people. In 2004 the dogs ended their dangerous rescue work and the breeding was taken over by the Barry Foundation, named for the most famous of the Saint Bernard dogs who personally rescued over 40 people.

Two St. Bernards rescuing a stranded traveler with monks and hospice in background by E.A. Odier. *Zentralbibliothek Solothurn [Public domain]*

The Magic Number

Christian theology is full of 3s. Some good. Some not so good. We believe in the Trinity, God in three persons. We do not believe in tritheism, three separate gods. A popular way to visualize the trinity is through the interwoven diagram known as the triquetra. Munus Triplex is the Latin phrase roughly translated "triple duty" referring to the threefold office of Christ as prophet, priest and king. The concept is first described by 4th century Christian historian Eusebius and later developed by John Calvin. Another 4th century Latin phrase, tertium quid, was the heretical idea that Jesus wasn't really human or divine but a unique mix of the two making him a kind of "third thing". There is ongoing theological debate about whether

people are made of two parts (body and spirit/soul) or three parts (body, soul and spirit). Trichotomists who presume three parts, cite Hebrews 4:12 which says that the spirit and soul can be divided by the word of God. Finally, the term Paschal Triduum refers to the three days of Jesus' death.

Dogmatic Sacrophagus c. 350AD (earliest known depiction of the trinity) from Vatican Museum.
Gx872op [Public domain]

Space Window

On July 21, 1974, the three astronauts from Apollo 11 presented a 2 3/8 inch piece of moon rock to the National Cathedral in Washington, D.C. Officially known as "Piece 230 of Apollo 11 rock no. 10057", the rock is incased in a nitrogen filled container of steel and glass. It is the centerpiece of what has become known as the space window, a three paneled stained-glass window depicting a somewhat abstract representation of the cosmos. There is an inscription at the base of the window with the words from Job 22.12, "Is not God in the height of Heaven?" Curiously enough, there is

another space themed addition to the National Cathedral. Near the top of the northwest tower there is a grotesque (not to be confused with a gargoyle) of Darth Vader that was added in the 1980s. Note that a grotesque is a more general term for a decorative figure while a gargoyle specifically serves as a drainage spout.

Space Window with Moon Rock in the center. *Tim Evanson [CC BY-SA 2.0 (https://creativecommons.org/licenses/by-sa/2.0)]*

51

Three Cages

Close up of the empty cages. Foto Fitti [CC BY-SA 3.0 (https://creativecommons.org/licenses/by-sa/3.0)]

St. Lambert's Church in Münster, Germany has three very macabre decorations hanging high up on its steeple. On January 22, 1536 the remains of three men were hung in cages to rot as a reminder and a warning. The now empty cages held the remains of Jan of Leiden, Bernhard Knipperdolling and Bernhard Kretching, leaders of what historians call the Münster Rebellion. In a tense political and religious climate a group of radical Anabaptists seized control from both Catholics and Protestants proclaiming the city to be the new Jerusalem. The former bishop of the city, a wealthy man named Franz von Waldeck besieged the city for over a year. Inside Münster, Jan of Leiden, the leader of the rebellion increasing exerted control over a starving and desperate group of a few thousand people. He instituted polygamy (personally marrying 16 women), had himself declared king and claimed to have visions from heaven. When von Waldeck's siege eventually succeeded, he had Leiden and two surviving leaders imprisoned then tortured and killed before hanging their bodies in the cages that remain today.

Touchdown, Terminator, Hug Me Jesus

Solid Rock Church just outside of Cincinnati, Ohio is well known to travelers along I-75. The megachurch's property runs alongside the northbound side of the interstate. In 2004, Solid Rock commissioned a statue of Jesus that would be seen by passersby. *King of Kings* was a 62-foot-tall statue of Jesus emerging with arms raised high from a man-made pond. Its prominence earned it a few nicknames including Touchdown Jesus and Big Butter Jesus thanks to a comedian who thought its yellowish hue looked like a carving you might see at a state fair. Unfortunately, in 2010 the statue was struck by lighting and burned everything except the metal framing underneath. Images of the engulfed statue earned it a new nickname, Terminator Jesus. In 2012 a new statue *Lux Mundi*, Latin for "Light of the World", took its place. The 52-foot-tall Jesus is standing upright with arms outstretched toward the interstate. It has been nicknamed Hug Me Jesus.

Lux Mundi, aka Hug Me Jesus. *Traveler100 [CC BY-SA 4.0 (https://creativecommons.org/licenses/by-sa/4.0)]*

Hidden Church

(above) Interior View. *Remi Mathis [CC BY-SA 3.0 (https://creativecommons.org/licenses/by-sa/3.0)]*

(right) Our Lord in the Attic, Exterior View. *A. T. Rooswinkel [Public domain]*

In the Netherlands during the 17th and 18th century the only official churches were Reformed churches. But there were other, hidden places where Catholics and Mennonites and other religious minorities could gather. They were tolerated so long as they were discrete and could not be identified as churches from the outside. In Dutch they are called *Schuilkerken* "hidden church" or sometimes in rural areas *Schuurkerken* "barn church". From the outside, most of these churches would look like houses or businesses. The famed Dutch painter Vermeer converted to Catholicism and was married in a barn that served as the Catholic church in his small village. One particularly well-preserved example of these hidden churches is the Ons' Lieve Heer op Solder (in English "Our Lord in the Attic") which was built in 1630. The top three floors were converted into a Catholic Church in the 1660s. In 1888 it was converted into a museum which is still open to visitors.

Headless Saints

A cephalophore is saint who is depicted holding their own head in their hands symbolizing their martyrdom by beheading. There are more than 100 known cephalophores. While all cephalophores died by beheading, some died more slowly than others. The most famous example is Saint Denis, who was the bishop of Paris during the 3rd century.

Woodcut of St. Denis, 1826. *Public Domain.*

According to legend, after he was beheaded, Denis picked up his head and preached the gospel as he walked several miles through the city before finally dying. Many were said to have converted at the miraculous event. At the site of his burial is the Basilica of Saint Denis, which is also famous for being the burial place for nearly every French monarch. Unlike Denis, not all cephalophores were completely decapitated. Saint Piatus who also lived during the 3rd century was an evangelist to Chartres, Frances and Tournai, Belgium. Piatus had the top of his head sliced off and is often depicted holding a small part of his head in his hands.

One Tough Saint

Saint Erasmus was the Bishop of Formia, Italy until his martyrdom in 303AD. Because of his boldness in evangelism, he is said to have faced a series of particularly cruel attempts to make him recant his faith. He was beaten, hanged, placed in a pit of poisonous snakes, dipped in tar and set on fire, made to wear a white-hot metal cloak, put inside a barrel with spikes and rolled down a hill, placed in chains and left to starve. Somehow none of these killed him and

each time that God preserved him more people came to faith. He is often portrayed holding a windlass wrapped with his entrails representing the method which finally succeeded in killing him. His reputation of being especially protected by God also includes an account of when he continued to preach despite nearly being struck by lightning. For this reason Saint Erasmus, also known as Saint Elmo, has long served as the patron saint of sailors seeking protection. One supposed sign of his presence during a thunder storm was a glowing ball of light that would sometimes appear near the mast of a ship during bad thunderstorms. This meteorological phenomenon which is a form of plasma came to be known as Saint Elmo's Fire.

Painting of Saint Erasmus from 1520. *Wolfgang Sauber [CC BY-SA 4.0 (https://creativecommons.org/licenses/by-sa/4.0)]*

The Immovable Ladder

There is a wooden ladder outside of a church in Jerusalem that hasn't moved in almost 300 years. The Immovable Ladder as it is known is symbolic of an uneasy relationship between various Christian communities all claiming control over the most holy sites in Jerusalem. In 1757 when Jerusalem was ruled by the Ottoman Empire, a decree established the *status quo* granting ownership of nine holy sites to various Christian, Jewish or Muslim communities. One of these sites is the Church of the Holy Sepulcher which is built above the place of Jesus' crucifixion and his burial. Its

Immovable Ladder visible in a 1914 photograph. *American Colony (Jerusalem). Photo Dept. Public domain.*

ownership is claimed by at least six Christian communities. Because of the status quo no group can make changes or move anything without the consent of the other groups. This includes moving a ladder that has sat on a ledge above the entrance to the church since at least 1727. Over the years a few attempts have been made to move or destroy the ladder, and it has technically been moved at least twice to allow for repairs. But it still remains as a symbol of the *status quo.*

Dominus Flevit

There is a church in Jerusalem with perhaps the only chicken-themed tile mosaic in the world. The mosaic is at the foot of the altar in this small church. It is fitting for this image of a hen with wings outstretched over her chicks to be in this particular place. Behind the altar is a window with a panoramic view of the temple mount. The church is built mid-way down the western hillside of the Mount of Olives on the way into Jerusalem. It was at this site on Palm Sunday where Jesus stopped and upon seeing the temple, he wept over the city (Luke 19). In fact, the name of the church, Dominus Flevit, in Latin means "The Lord wept". The inspiration for the chicken mosaic comes Luke 13:34 in which Jesus says, "O Jerusalem, Jerusalem, the city that kills the prophets and stones those who are sent to it! How often would I have gathered your children together as a hen gathers her brood under her wings, and you were not willing!"

(above) Tile Mosaic on altar of Dominus Flevit. *Public Domain.*

(right) Looking out the window behind the altar with a view of the Temple Mount.
Berthold Werner [CC BY-SA 3.0 (https://creativecommons.org/licenses/by-sa/3.0)]

Quick-thinking Mother

Origen of Alexandria (184-253) is one of the most significant early church fathers. While he was sometimes controversial, he was also highly influential. He was an important voice in the early development of the doctrine of the trinity and was one of the first to propose the ransom theory of atonement, which states that God paid a ransom to Satan to redeem his people. But he also had some strange ideas about souls and has often been accused of being a being a universalist. Long after his death he was condemned as a

Origen as an old man. *Public Domain.*

heretic for his more outlandish ideas. Nonetheless, he was and remains a significant voice from the early church. But all of his accomplishments might have been lost had it not been for his quick-thinking mother who saved his life in a strange way. Origen's family were Christians and his father was an outspoken believer who was condemned during a period of intense persecution. Origen wanted to join his father and be martyred but his mom hid all of his clothes. Origen was apparently unwilling to face martyrdom with nothing to wear and was thus spared by his mother's actions.

Jerome's Lion

Engraving of Saint Jerome by Albrecht Durer, 1514. *Albrecht Dürer [CC0]*

St Jerome (347-420) is known as one of the four great teachers of the church along with Augustine, Ambrose and Gregory the Great. He is most famous for translating the Greek and Hebrew bible into Latin, which was the common language spoken at the time. In fact, this bible is called the "Vulgate" which means common. A popular subject of many medieval and Renaissance artists, Jerome is often depicted at work in his study with a few symbolic items prominently placed nearby including a skull representing both death and wisdom, a cardinal's hat representing his authority in the church, a book representing his role as bible translator and a lion! The lion is a reference to an almost certainly embellished if not altogether fictitious story about Jerome bravely removing a thorn from a lion's paw and subsequently inviting the lion to stay as a companion at his monastery. The lion, like all residents of the monastery, was required to work and was given the task of guarding the monastery's donkey. The story first appeared in the 13th century book *Golden Legend* which is a collection of hagiographies, or saint biographies.

Not that Bozo

Anselm of Canterbury. *Public Domain.*

Anselm of Canterbury (1033-1109) was a noteworthy intellectual leader in the church. As a monk he spent most of his life at Bec monastery in France eventually becoming its abbot. Under Anselm, Bec became one of the most important places of learning in all of Europe. Following the Norman Invasion, Anselm was installed as the Archbishop of Canterbury where he continued his work as a theologian. Anselm is best known for developing the satisfaction theory of the atonement. He was not content with the previously held idea that Christ paid a debt to Satan to set us free. Anselm believed that Satan was owed nothing and that Christ's death satisfies the debt owed to God. Anselm also attempted to prove the existence of God by reason alone. He theorized that God is that of which nothing greater can be imagined. To present his argument he wrote a fictional dialogue between himself and his successor at Bec. The younger abbot often appears somewhat simple-minded asking questions and easily losing arguments to Anselm. The foolish abbot's name was Boso, though it appears to be a coincidence and not related to the contemporary term "bozo".

Skate Church

Church buildings all over the United States are being repurposed as congregations dwindle and church attendance wanes. One church is now a photography studio in Philadelphia and another is a college dorm in Madison, Wisconsin. In

Church of Eight Wheels. *Image Courtesy of Church of Eight Wheels.*

Charleston, South Carolina another has become a restaurant and candy store. Several churches including one in Pittsburgh are now breweries. Another is a bookstore in New York. Several former churches are now event venues or private homes. But all is not lost. There are always new churches that open just as there are churches that close. Sometimes they overlap. For example, the Church of 8 Wheels in San Francisco is a skating rink housed in the former Sacred Heart Catholic Church which closed in 2004. On the other side of the country is Christ Central Church in Charlotte, North Carolina which meets in a former skating rink.

Vrontados Rocket War

The Greek Orthodox Church has a unique way of celebrating Easter. On the Saturday night before Easter congregants gather around 11pm. During the service all of the lights are turned off until midnight when the priest with a single candle in hand declares that Christ has risen. Then one by one

Celebrants shooting off rockets.
Dimitris Tachynakos [CC BY-SA 4.0 (https://creativecommons.org/licenses/by-sa/4.0)]

everyone's candle is lit and remains lit as families leave the church and head home. Soon afterward celebration rings throughout the city. Bells are rung and fireworks light up the sky. In one Greek town, they take this tradition to the next level. Instead of just shooting off a few fireworks and calling it a night, two neighboring churches in Vrontados on the island of Chios shoot off tens of thousands of fireworks at each other's bell towers. All in good fun, the goal is to ring the bell of the other church the most times. At the end of the night each group claims victory and agrees to battle again next year. This rocket war has been a tradition for over 200 years.

The Iconic Mr. Rogers

Mister Rogers is an icon of American children's television. And one Massachusetts church has taken it one step further by literally creating an icon of Mister Rogers. Icons have a long, complicated history. Common in the Eastern church, icons are most often not a part of Protestant traditions. Icons are a stylized image of a person, angel or event that is portrayed in a particular fashion such as to evoke veneration or reverence. Icons are not meant to be worshiped. This particular icon of Mister Rogers shows him in his trademark sweater with a golden halo and three simple words: gentle, kind and true. It is by the pew Rogers frequented at St. Paul's Episcopal Church in Nantucket. Rogers owned a cottage on the island and was a regular congregant when he was in town. If you happen to be visiting the church you might also be interested to see a more familiar form of church art. St. Paul's is also home to several authentic Tiffany stained glass windows.

(above) Mr. Rogers Icon. Artist unknown. *Photograph by Father Max Wolf, courtesy of St. Paul's Episcopal Church.*

(right) Tiffany Stained Glass Windows in rear of the church. *Photograph by Martin McKerrow, courtesy of St. Paul's Episcopal Church.*

Codex Amiatinus

The Codex Amiatinus, the earliest surviving complete manuscript of the Latin Vulgate is considered to be one of the greatest works of Anglo-Saxon Britain. It was completed in the late 7th century at the twin abbeys of Saint Peter and Saint Paul in Monkwearmouth–Jarrow in Northumbria, England. Originally, three copies were made: one for each of the abbeys and a third, Codex Amiatinus, was intended as a gift for

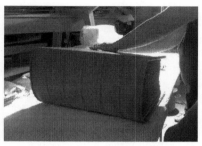

Codex Amiatinus being examined. *Remi Mathis [CC BY-SA 4.0 (https://creativecommons.org/licenses/by-sa/4.0)]*

Pope Gregory II. While only fragments remain of the other manuscripts, Codex Amiatinus is wonderfully preserved. Despite being dedicated as a gift to the pope it never made it to Rome and instead wound up in a Tuscan abbey near Monte Amiata, for which it is named. At some point the words dedicating the bible to the pope were erased and a fake dedication was added. This false dedication went unnoticed for over a thousand years. One piece of evidence that led to undercovering the truth was the written remarks about the manuscript's creation by none other than the Venerable Bede who was a monk at the monastery when the copies were made. Besides it historical significance, what makes this particular bible special is its size. It is approximately 19 x 13 inches and 7 inches thick. It weighs over 75lbs. The 1030 vellum pages were made of animal skin from more than 500 calves. In order to raise enough livestock to produce all three original copies, the monasteries needed more than 2000 acres of land.

Wayfarer's Dole

There is a place in Winchester, England where if you ask, you'll be given a cup of beer and a morsel of bread for free. The Hospital of St. Cross is an Almshouse established around 1132 to provide care for poor men and feed over one hundred meals daily to others. It remains England's oldest charitable institution. The term hospital is used in the older sense of  hospitality or charity and not as a place of medical care. Tradition states that a monk from the Cluny Monastery in France was working at the almshouse and brought with him the practice known as the Wayfarer's Dole. At Cluny, monks would give out wine and bread to all who asked. The Hospital of St. Cross adapted the practice switching wine for beer, the preferred drink of England. Today, when visiting St. Cross, if you go to the Porter's Lodge and ask for the dole, you'll be given a bit of bread and a cup of local beer.

Hospital of St. Cross. *Johan Bakker [CC BY-SA 3.0 (https://creativecommons.org/licenses/by-sa/3.0)]*

(previous page) Wayfarer's Dole. *Public Domain.*

The Sweet Potato of Life

Every time the gospel goes to a new culture there is both freedom and responsibility to take the truth of the gospel to that culture in a way that they can understand. In Acts, Paul uses this tactic when speaking to philosophers on Mars Hill. One contemporary place where this is done is in bible translation. Trying to contextualize the heart of scripture into a culture and language that may not carry the same meaning can lead to some interesting choices. In Papua New Guinea, bread is not a staple of their diet. When it can be found, it is very expensive. In some communities they don't even have a word "bread" in their language. So, translators trying to convey the meaning of John 6:48 "I am the bread of life" chose another starchy food that is a staple of the local diet. In Papua New Guinea, Jesus is the sweet potato of life.

Dura-Europos

The oldest known church is a house church that dates back to around 240AD. The church was discovered in a former city of about 6,000 people along the banks of the Euphrates River known as Dura-Europos which is in modern day Syria. Around 256AD the town was conquered by an invading army. It's people were deported and the town was abandoned and buried by mud and sand preserving much of the original structures. In 1920, British soldiers were digging trenches and found a wall covered in paintings. Eventually archaeologists from Syria, France and Yale University began excavations. Many buildings were found including a synagogue and a church. Several frescoes were found inside the church including one of Christ as the Good Shepherd. The building had a baptistery as well as a room for about 70 people to gather. The Dura-Europos church is extremely important because it gives a glimpse of what the early church looked like before Christianity became the official religion of Rome. Many of the frescoes and other artifacts from the church are now housed at Yale although most are not on display in order to preserve their condition. Unfortunately, Dura-Europos is one of many sites almost completely destroyed by ISIS.

Dura Europas. *Johan Bakker [CC BY-SA 3.0 (https://creativecommons.org/licenses/by-sa/3.0)]*

Spark

John Wesley Carhart (1834-1914) was a Methodist minister with a number of interests. He wrote poetry, hymns, fiction, and historical books. He sold insurance and ran a printing press. He was involved in the temperance movement. After leaving ministry he went back to school and became a medical doctor and contributed to medical journals. Most notably though, he was an inventor. With help from his brother, a professor of physics at the University of Michigan, he built the first automobile in America. The steam-powered car he nicknamed "Spark" took its inaugural drive in September 1873 in Racine, Wisconsin where Carhart was pastor. "Spark" was coal powered, had two cylinders and weighed 1,100 pounds. It's top speed was less than 5mph. Steering was controlled by levers. Unfortunately, the car terrified horses and people and was officially banned by the city on October 20. Carhart dismantled the car and appears to have moved on to other things. He never lost interest in cars though, and in his later years was awarded several patents for tire designs.

Theologian Trading Cards

Trading cards have been popular since the late 1800s when tobacco companies began printing pictures and assorted trivia on the thick card-stock paper inserted in the packaging to protect the tobacco. Chewing gum companies would follow suit in the 1930s. Eventually the cards became a product in their own right with sports figures being the most common subject. More recently, popular card games like Pokémon have introduced a new kind of collectible trading card. There have also been cards produced to help military personnel to identify friendly and enemy aircraft. In 2012 a set of theologian trading cards was created by Norman Jeune III and published by Zondervan. There are 288 cards with a variety of theologians from contemporary thinkers, early church fathers, reformers and heretics. They are arranged on "teams" that help to broadly categorize each theologian. The back of the card includes a bit of biographical info and brief description of their contribution. You can pick up a set for about $20.

Priest Holes

During the reigns of Queen Elizabeth I (1558-1603) and King James I (1603-1625) there were several plots by Catholics to assassinate monarchs throughout Europe. In response England severely persecuted Catholics. In 1584, Parliament passed the Jesuit, etc. Act which required  all Catholic priests to leave the country or swear an oath of loyalty to the monarch. It also made it illegal to harbor priests. Despite the prohibition, some Catholic families went to great lengths to hide priests in their homes. They built secret hideouts called priest holes behind walls, under floors, in fireplaces, and many other places. The most prolific designer of priest holes was a Jesuit named Nicholas

Owen. His hiding spots were so well designed and so secret that some, such as one at Harvington Hall, were not discovered for nearly 300 years. Owen was eventually caught and tortured but never disclosed the locations of his work. He was canonized in the 1970s and is the patron saint of escape artists and illusionists.

(above) Priest Hole at Boscobel House.
Sjwells53 [CC BY-SA 3.0 (https://creativecommons.org/licenses/by-sa/3.0)]

(left) Nicholas Owen being tortured. Drawing by Gaspar Bouttats. *Public Domain.*

Wild Graveyard

Charleston, South Carolina is known as the Holy City because there are many big, beautiful historic churches. You can visit First Baptist, the oldest Baptist church in the south (founded 1682). Or visit Old St. Andrew's Parish Church, the oldest surviving church in the Carolinas (built 1706). You can see Mother Emanuel

Wild and overgrown graveyard at the Unitarian Church in Charleston. *Photograph by author.*

A.M.E. which is the oldest AME church in the south and the site a tragic mass shooting in 2015. You can see the pew George Washington sat in at St. Michael's. The Circular Congregation Church is one of the more interesting architectural buildings in the city and was the first church to introduce Sunday School in the Carolinas. Many of these churches also have historic graveyards. One of the more interesting historic graveyards belongs to the Unitarian Church. Designed as a garden cemetery by the wife of one of the church's first ministers, it is one of the oldest Unitarian graveyards in America with tombstones dating to the 1700's. What makes it so unique is quickly apparent to any visitor. Rather than well-manicured plots, the congregants have decided to allow the graveyard to grow wild and natural. Accessible during the day via a beautiful alleyway near the corner of King Street and Queen Street, it is also a popular stop during the evening ghost walk tours.

Beer Garden VBS

One of the most popular institutions in the American church is Vacation Bible School. In the 1990s nearly 80% of churches had a VBS program. Even today over half of the church in the US still offer a VBS with about 2.5 million kids attending every year. Most of these churches would be surprised to find out that one of the first places to host a VBS was a beer garden in the back of a saloon in New York City. In 1898 Virginia Sinclair Hawes rented the garden for six weeks in the mornings before patrons arrived for her "Everyday Bible School". The following year Mrs. Hawes' church, Baptist Church of the Epiphany, attempted against her advice to host the school in their church building. It should be noted that the children much preferred the more relaxed setting of the local beer garden to the formal church building. Nevertheless, within a few years the idea of churches hosting vacation bible schools spread, and by 1922 the first mass produced VBS curriculum was distributed. Today, you could walk right past the original site without ever knowing it was anything special. The former saloon at 324 E. 71st Street was replaced by an apartment building in the 1940s.

BAPTIST CHURCH OF THE EPIPHANY, MADISON AVENUE AND EAST 64TH STREET.

Epiphany Baptist Church. *Public Domain.*

Laps Are For Writing

Image of Ezra in Codex Amiatinus.
Public Domain.

Desks would seem like a good sturdy surface upon which to write, but not apparently in medieval culture. At least that is what you might conclude based on medieval art. In many pictures from this time monks or other religious figures, especially the gospel writers, are seen hard at work writing and transcribing texts. There is often a table present but only as a place to hold the inkwell. The person doing the writing is seen with the book or scroll in his lap diligently writing away. One of the best illustrations of this is from the late 7th century Codex Amiatinus, one of the earliest complete copies of the Latin Vulgate. In it there is a depiction of Ezra at work copying with the book in his lap despite a perfectly good desk nearby. The 13th century Burney Manuscript shows three of the four gospel writers with book and quill in their lap. John who is depicted in his chair ready to write but with no book in hand apparently waiting for divine inspiration. Another example is the 15th century Armenian Gospels on display at the Met depict the same idea. While it is very unlikely that medieval monks wrote with books in their laps, it is a strange bit of artistic license that isn't entirely understood.

Pater Noster Church

Jesus taught his disciples to pray what has come to be known as the Lord's Prayer beginning with the words, "Our Father". The location where this takes places is only listed as happening at a "certain place" (a very vague description, indeed) according to the gospel of Luke. Tradition locates this "certain place" in a cave somewhere near the top of the Mount of Olives. Since Luke and the other gospel writers offer little detail, we have instead to thank Helena, the mother of Constantine, the first Christian emperor of Rome. She went about trying to identify every holy place in and around Jerusalem in the 4th century. While the site has fallen in and out of use over the centuries, it is currently home to a Carmelite Monastery and a church known as the Pater Noster, the Latin translation of "Our Father". Adorning the church walls are versions of the Lord's Prayer translated into 140 different languages.

Wall with copies of the Lord's Prayer. *Britchi Mirela [CC BY-SA 4.0 (https://creativecommons.org/licenses/by-sa/4.0)]*

(previous page) Pater Noster Church circa 1950. *Willem van de Poll [CC0]*

Underwater Church

Church ruins can be extraordinary places to visit. Strolling through the beautiful remains offers a glimpse of past splendor. But not all church ruins are on land. Several are buried under water, often the unfortunate casualties of early twentieth century dams. There are dozens of churches fully or partially submerged in man-made lakes. Occasionally though, churches do resurface. Apostle Santiago is a 16th century church in Chiapas, Mexico that emerged during a drought in 2015. Often, a partially submerged church becomes a curiosity and local landmark. Probably the most common and beautiful site is a stone bell tower emerging from the water. And there are a few of these. The most picturesque is in Lake Reschen in Graun, Switzerland. When the lake freezes, it is possible to walk out to the tower. The most impressive is the bell tower of St. Nicholas Church in Kalyazin, Russia. Built in 1800 and flooded to make way for a hydroelectric dam in 1939, it rises nearly 250 feet above the water. Prior to the dam's construction the rest of the church which dates back several centuries was dismantled and the bells were removed from the tower. Only the tower remained. Today it is a popular tourist attraction with a tiny man-made island and small dock allowing for visitors. The Russian Orthodox Church still uses the tower a few times a year to host a worship service.

Lake Reschen Belltower. *Zairon [CC BY-SA 4.0*
(https://creativecommons.org/licenses/by-sa/4.0)]

(previous page) St. Nicholas Belltower. *Vladimir Pakhomov [CC BY-SA 3.0*
(https://creativecommons.org/licenses/by-sa/3.0)]

Airport Chapel

At Boston's Logan International Airport, in between terminal B and Terminal C lies the appropriately named, Our Lady of the Airways chapel. It is the nation's first airport chapel. Originally built in a different site inside the airport in 1951, it was relocated to make way for expansion in 1965. In the 1960's several other airports built their own chapels beginning with Our Lady of the Skies at JFK Airport in New York. The first chapels were built by the Catholic dioceses in major cities to serve airport employees, not passengers. Later, Protestant chapels began to appear at major airports for passengers and employees. Today instead of single faith chapels, most airports host interfaith spaces with a variety of religious symbols such as the chapel at Charlotte Douglas International Airport. Others are simple rooms devoid of symbols such as the one at San Francisco International Airport which is designed for quiet reflection rather than to hold religious services. One unique problem for older chapels is that many are located before security checkpoints and are more difficult to access for employees and passengers. The chapel at Seattle Tacoma International Airport was built near the ticket counters in 1971. It was closed from 2015-2017 but reopened largely due to requests of Buddhist and Muslim groups. They have plans to build a second location on the other side of security by 2021.

Ice Cream Truck Ministry

In the small town of Arley, Alabama there is a church that has a unique way of blessing the community. In January 2018, Arley First Baptist Church began the process of creating the very first ice cream truck ministry. The small church was able to make that dream a reality later that year. The town which is about an hour north of Birmingham has a population of less than 500. The church was looking for a way to practice what they preached, especially Jesus' command from Mark 12:31 to love their neighbors. Providing ice cream free of charge to adults and kids is their way of bringing above and beyond joy to their community.

Jedediah's Three Sons

Jedediah Morse (1761-1826) studied theology at Yale under Jonathan Edwards. After graduation he became a minister. Controversially, Morse believed and sometimes preached that the Illuminati from France were attempting to infiltrate the United States through various political, social and religious movements. Despite this particular belief, he was well regarded in society and was friends with such noteworthy people as John Adams and Noah Webster. Jedediah was best known for his work as a geographer. His book *American Geography* which was updated annually became the definitive text for decades. For this reason, he is often called the father of American geography. Jedediah was also an actual father and is perhaps best remembered because of his sons, the eldest in particular.

Richard, the youngest son was a geographer and often assisted his father. The middle son, Sidney studied theology at Yale and became a geographer as well as an inventor. Sidney's final years were spent working on an invention he called a bathyometer, a vessel designed for deep sea exploration. Jedediah Morse's oldest son Samuel was a painter of some renown, but you probably recognize his name for another reason. Following the sudden death of his wife, Samuel was heartbroken that he didn't receive word of her illness faster and invented a device to more quickly pass along information. The device was the single wire telegraph using a simple code of dots and dashes known today as Morse code.

(above) Samuel Morse from Archives of American Art. *Public domain.*

(previous page) Jedediah Morse painting by Samuel Morse. *Public Domain.*

Wonder Worker

Icon of Gregory Thaumaturgus. Public Domain.

A Thaumaturge is a saint who was especially known for working magic or miracles. The word comes from two Greek words thauma meaning wondrous thing and ergon meaning work. There have been many such wonder workers in church history. Ambrose of Optina (1812-1891) was said to have the power to heal as well as clairvoyance. Gerald Majella was an 18th century Italian who is said to have brought a boy back to life, could appear in two places at once and walked on water to lead fisherman safely through a storm. Probably the most famous of these saintly wonder workers is Gregory of Neocaesarea (213-270AD) commonly known as Gregory Thaumaturgus. He is credited with healing many illnesses, settling a dispute between brothers by diving a pond in two, and moving boulders by his command. Gregory is supposed to have been asked to prevent a river from flooding. He did so by planting his staff in the ground and commanding the water not to go past it. Immediately the staff sprouted into a tree and the river ceased flooding. Most amazingly, Gregory is said to have converted a pagan priest by giving a permission slip to Satan. The story is that Gregory took shelter from a storm in a pagan temple and spend the night in prayer. The next day, the pagan priest found that the temple oracle, a demon in disguise, could not enter. Gregory wrote the note allowing the demon back in, but the priest in awe at the authority Gregory had over the demon immediately converted to Christianity.

Seminary President and NFL Coach

Most NFL head coaches work their way up by coaching at a lower level and gradually gaining promotions and responsibility. One of the more common first jobs for aspiring coaches is as a graduate assistant working with a college team while completing a masters. It can take ten years or more to work through the college coaching system to be offered that first assistant coaching job in the NFL. Then another ten years working through the ranks to be offered a head coaching job. This makes Frank Reich, current head coach of the Indianapolis Colts, an outlier. Frank Reich was a long-time backup quarterback in the NFL (1985-1998). After his playing career was over, Reich did go to grad school, but it wasn't at a major college. He went to seminary. Reich briefly served as a pastor at Ballantyne Presbyterian Church and then as the president of his alma mater, Reformed Theological Seminary in Charlotte, NC. Only then at 46 did Reich decide to take a shot at becoming an NFL coach. His first job was as an unpaid intern with the Colts. After twelve years of working as an assistant coach, the former seminary president was announced as the head coach of the Indianapolis Colts in 2018.

Unity Temple

Frank Lloyd Wright (1867-1959) is one of the most famous American architects of all time. His use of unconventional materials, dramatic design elements and attention to detail (going so far as to design cutlery and linens for each home) are recognizable even by non-architects today. He designed such grand structures as the Guggenheim Museum in New York City and amazing homes like Fallingwater, a house built atop a waterfall in rural Pennsylvania. In addition, he designed office buildings, small "affordable" homes and several religious buildings. He designed everything from a synagogue shaped like a pyramid in Pennsylvania to an entire Methodist college in Florida. His most famous religious building was his first. Unity Temple in Oak Park, Illinois was the Unitarian church that Wright himself attended. After a fire destroyed the original structure, he was commissioned to design a new meeting space which was completed in 1909. It is widely considered to be the first modern building due to its thorough use of reinforced concrete and a design language which heavily influenced subsequent architects. The original budget for the project was $45,000, but after delays the final cost was $90,000. It has been a historic landmark since 1971. A two-year restoration begun in 2015 cost $23 million. Tours are available every day but Sunday when the congregation still gathers.

Unity Temple, 1967. Historic American Buildings Survey. *Public Domain.*

Royal Peculiar

A Royal Peculiar is a uniquely British term. It refers to a church or parish in the Church of England that doesn't fall under the jurisdiction of a bishop but is directly controlled by the monarch. The idea dates back almost a thousand years. There are several throughout the UK, with most concentrated in the city of London. St Peter ad Vincula is the first of two Royal Peculiars in the Tower of London and is the burial site of many famous people executed at the Tower including Anne Boleyn. Elsewhere in London, Temple Church is the English headquarters of the Knights Templar and the location where the booming organ music for the soundtrack to the movie *Interstellar* was recorded. The most famous Royal Peculiar is the Collegiate Church of St. Peter, more commonly known as Westminster Abbey. One of the most unique Royal Peculiars is the Chapel of St. Mary Undercroft, a crypt chapel built below the former Westminster Palace, completed in 1365 and restored in 1870. It has served as a chapel, a dining room and even as a stable for Oliver Cromwell's horses. It is also the site where the suffragette Emily Wilding Davison hid in a broom closet the night before the 1911 census so that she could record her address as the House of Commons in protest.

(above) Temple Church in 1890. *Public Domain.*

(previous page) Westminster Abbey in 1804. *Public Domain.*

Butt Song from Hell

Hieronymous Bosch (1450-1516) is a famous Dutch painter who is known for his wildly fantastic depictions of religious imagery. He rarely explained his works, so interpretations are up for debate. His most famous piece of artwork is a triptych, or three paneled painting that can be folded closed. *The Garden of Earthly Delights* when folded closed shows God at work in creation with a giant sphere on a stark black background. When opened the left panel depicts Adam and Eve in the Garden, possibly at the moment God introduces her to him. The large center panel shows many nude figures in various slightly suggestive acts interspersed with both fantastic and real creatures. Oh yeah, there are also people carrying around gigantic fruit. Interpretations of this panel vary from carnal lust to an alternate reality wherein humanity never committed the first sin. The right panel takes a decidedly dark tone depicting hell with the same level of fantasy only more distorted and contorted. The background is burning. Beasts both real and distorted are devouring people. And people are crucified on musical instruments. Just below that a choir is singing a song with the music written on a man's bare buttocks. It is a thoroughly revolting picture of hell. In case you were wondering what hell sounds like, in 2014 some musicians noticed that you could actually read the music and so they recorded it. There are now several versions of the melody known as Bosch's 600 year old butt song from hell.

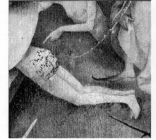

Garden of Earthly Delights, right pannel and close up (previous page). *Public Domain.*

(previous page) Portrait of Bosch in 1585. *Public Domain.*

The American Colony

MR. H. G. SPAFFORD

Many people are familiar with the sad story of Horatio Spafford that inspired the song *It is Well with My Soul.* Shortly after fire wiped out much of the successful lawyer's investments, Spafford planned a trip to England with his four daughters and wife Anna to benefit her health and to visit his friend Dwight Moody. At the last minute Horatio was unable to make the trip. Mid-voyage their ship collided with another ship and sank almost instantly. Anna was pulled unconscious from the wreckage that claimed the lives of their four daughters. While making the Atlantic crossing to join his mourning wife Horatio penned the hymn as he passed the spot that claimed the daughters' lives.

What is not often told is the rest of the Spafford's story. Horatio and Anna went on to have three more children. Sadly, another child died of scarlet fever. Rumors in the Presbyterian church where Horatio was an elder began to spread about how God may be punishing them. Distraught, they left the church to found a community modeled after the early Christians and moved to Jerusalem. Over the years the American Colony, as their group came to be known, began to shift their beliefs adopting a more fervent Messianic tone. Nevertheless, they were well received for their social work and orphan care among local Christians, Muslims and Jews. The Colony eventually disbanded, but an offshoot begun by the Spaffords' eldest surviving daughter continues this work and provides care to over 30,000 children per year.

American Colony in Jerusalem, circa 1920. *Matson Collection, Public Domain.*

(previous page) Portait of Horatio Spafford. *Public Domain.*

Parking Space 23

If you head to the beautiful 12th century St. Giles Cathedral in Edinburgh, you should check out the intricate wood carvings in Thistle Chapel. And don't forget the stained-glass window honoring poet Robbie Burns (famously celebrated for his love of Haggis). But most assuredly you will want to step out back to visit parking space 23. There you will find a plaque indicating it as the final resting place of John Knox, the Scottish reformer and founder of the Presbyterian Church. Knox was a priest who converted from Catholicism in 1544. After spending time as a prisoner and in exile, Knox eventually returned to Scotland in 1559 as the leading reformer. He marched into St. Giles proclaiming it to be a Protestant church, was installed as the minister and promptly went about stripping away all signs of Catholicism. He remained as the minister for another 13 years. Shortly before Knox died he supposedly requested to be buried within 20 feet of the church. In accordance with his request, he was buried on November 26, 1572 in the church graveyard. The problem is that by then the graveyard had become so overfilled with bodies that bones would pop out after the rain. The graveyard was actually closed for new burials a decade before Knox's death. Eventually the graveyard was emptied to make room for a new parliament building in 1639. Knox's remains alone were left to honor his request. During the 1970s the former graveyard was paved to add parking spaces between the church and the parliament building. Parking space 23 which is still in use remains the burial site of one of the most significant men in church history.

St. Giles Cathedral. *Chabe01 [CC BY-SA 4.0 (https://creativecommons.org/licenses/by-sa/4.0)]*

(previous page) Parking Space 23. *Kim Traynor [CC BY-SA 3.0 (https://creativecommons.org/licenses/by-sa/3.0)]*

The Real Emeth

C. S. Lewis is perhaps the best known Christian writer of all time. But there has been criticism of some of his theology. One minor character he created seems to have stirred up the most controversy. Emeth is the Calormen soldier in *The Last Battle* who volunteers to meet the (false) god of his people only to find himself welcomed into eternity by Aslan the true god. This character has long been seen by critics of Lewis as permitting a kind of universalism. Whatever your opinion, what you may not know is that Lewis is believed to have based this character on a real person. Professor Mahmoud Manzalaoui (1924-2015) studied under Lewis at Oxford from 1945-1948 and had begun attending meetings that Lewis presided over in the Socratic Club, a society for the rational discussion of the Christian religion. Manzalaoui an Egyptian Muslim, was at the time working on 18th century English translations of Arabic texts under Lewis's guidance. While Lewis never said who inspired the character, Manzalaoui somewhat sheepishly concludes that his presence in Lewis's life likely contributed to the inspiration of Emeth. You can find Manzalaoui's comments in the footnotes of his contribution (pp. 205-223) to the book *Journey Into Narnia* by Kathryn Lindskoog.

Skellig Michael: Jedi Temple

If you watched the movie *Star Wars: The Last Jedi*, then you might remember the remote water planet Ahch-To with its rocky islands and steep terrain. One island in particular, Temple Island was the birthplace of the Jedi Order and

Skellig Michael cemetary and distinctive beehive hut.
Jibi44 [CC BY-SA 3.0 (http://creativecommons.org/licenses/by-sa/3.0/)]

the site of the first Jedi temple. It looked like the set designers did a great job of creating a dramatic, remote ancient monastery. But they didn't build it. Instead, they chose a very real 6th century monastery. Skellig Michael, off the coast of Ireland was used from the 6th to the 12th century as an Augustinian monastery. The beehive shaped buildings from the movie are the very well preserved cells where the monks lived. Today, Skellig Michael is a UNESCO world heritage site and is accessible by no more than 180 tourists per day in the summer months. Visiting is not for the faint of heart. The seas are rough. The 600 stairs are steep and slippery, and there are no handrails.

Divine Mercy Jesus Statue

Have you ever wanted to step inside the heart of Jesus? Thanks to a group of Catholics at Divine Mercy Hills in the Philippines, you can. The group which is part of a small movement within Catholicism, holds a special reverence for Christ's endless goodness and attempts to show mercy to others. The movement can be traced back to a Polish nun who had visions and conversations with Jesus including a vision in 1931 in which Jesus appeared in white robes with red rays emanating from his heart representing his divine mercy. In the vision, Jesus asked the nun to paint the image and have it venerated all over the world. On a Philippine hillside overlooking

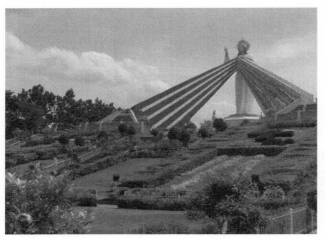

Divine Mercy Shrine. *Tin2little [CC BY-SA 3.0 (https://creativecommons.org/licenses/by-sa/3.0)]*

a picturesque bay, the group built a 50-foot statue of Jesus with red rays emanating from his heart. Visitors can walk up a staircase hidden in the rays to step into the very heart of Jesus, where a small chapel was built. Photos are not allowed inside, but a priest is present with the eucharist and

John Wesley, Electrotherapist

John Wesley (1704-1791) is most famous for founding the movement that would become known as Methodism. What is less well known is that he was also a pioneer in a new medical technique known as electrotherapy, the use of electric shock for treating illnesses. In 1747, he attended a demonstration of electricity and spent the next few years reading about this new subject and its medical benefits. In 1756, he purchased a device that could provide a static electric shock and began to experiment, first testing it as a curative for himself

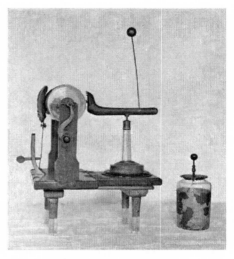

Wesley's Electical Machine.
Wellcome Collection, Public Domain.

with great success. Eventually he would purchase several more devices for the free medical clinics he established throughout London. He reported in his journal that hundreds and possibly thousands had been cured of diseases ranging from epilepsy to toothaches with no record of anyone being harmed. He also published several medical books advocating the virtues of electrotherapy, including *The Desideratum: Or, Electricity made Plain and Useful by a Lover of Mankind and of Common Sense*. He did all of this without ever obtaining a license to practice medicine. He considered doctors and pharmacists greedy men who abhorred such an inexpensive cure as electricity. ***Note, many health care professionals today consider electrotherapy to be torture.*

Homunculus Jesus

In classical art, there are numerous depictions of the infant Jesus with his mother Mary. In the early Middle Ages baby Jesus was often intentionally made to look like a miniature middle-aged man. The reason has to do with a widely held belief at the time that Jesus was born fully mature. Rather than try to portray a realistic Jesus, artists attempted to portray this in their art. Depictions show him as fully formed and yet still child-sized in a style known as homunculus (lit. "little man"). More often than not this led to childlike features mixed with adult features such as balding. Eventually as artists were commissioned to paint actual babies in nonreligious art, more lifelike depictions of the infant Jesus came to be preferred as well.

Virgin and Child with Saints. 13th century. Berlinghiero Berlinghieri. [*CC0]*
Public Domain.

(previous page) Madonna and Child with Two Angels. 13th century.
Duccio di Buoninsegna. *Public domain.*

Bathroom Graffiti

What is written on the walls of bathrooms is generally not the sort of thing that should be discussed in public. But any good archaeologist will tell you that its exactly this sort of place to look to get a glimpse of an earlier time. Here are two brief examples. There is a former monastery in Tepoztlán, Mexico that was being converted into a museum. During renovations, workers uncovered some poems scratched into the walls of the old bathrooms that date back to the 1840s. One poem reads, "No one can deny me, that in the world there is no pleasure greater than eating, and evacuating with measure." Around the same time on the other side of the world, the Vatican was doing some renovations to build a new apartment for the pope. One of the rooms being repurposed happened to be the bathroom of an especially worldly Cardinal named Bernardo Dovizi of Bibbiena (1470-1520). Dovizi had his friend, the famous Renaissance painter Raphael decorate the bathroom walls with graphic art, some of which has been since defaced or painted over. The pope does not use this room and its doors are almost always locked.

Tepoztlan bathroom stalls with writing barely visible. *PetrohsW [CC BY-SA 4.0 (https://creativecommons.org/licenses/by-sa/4.0)]*

Eugene Peterson, Athlete

Eugene Peterson (1932-2018) was a pastor, poet, theologian, author and more. He spent 29 years as pastor at Christ Our King Presbyterian Church in Bel Air, Maryland. For most of the next decade he was Professor of Spiritual Theology at Regent College in Vancouver, British Columbia. During this time,

Peterson (front) preparing to receive the batton. *Courtesy of Seattle Pacific University.*

he began the work for which he is most well-known, *The Message*, a down to earth translation of the Bible. Peterson was a prolific author who loved poetry, and his books could make even a seemingly boring topic come alive with visually rich imagery. The titles give a hint of his genius. One of Peterson's books is about the prophet Jeremiah, an important but frequently glossed over biblical character. Peterson's book is called *Run with the Horses: The Quest for Life at Its Best*. In naming the book, Peterson draws on God's words to the prophet in Jeremiah 12:5 (MSG), "So, Jeremiah, if you're worn out in this footrace with men, what makes you think you can race against horses..." It is a compelling image of a challenge to live life well and one that Peterson knew from personal experience. What most people don't know is that Eugene Peterson was himself an excellent runner. At Seattle Pacific College, he was part of a 4x440 relay team that placed third nationally in 1952.

World's Tallest Churches

While most of the world's tallest churches are in Europe, there are tall churches all over. The tallest church in Europe and the world champion at 530ft is Ulm Minster in Germany. Africa's tallest church at 518ft is Our Lady of Peace Basilica in Ivory Coast. The tallest church in North America at 423ft is St. Joseph's Oratory in Montreal, which has a wall full of thousands of crutches that people left behind after being healed. In South America, the tallest church is Brazil's Cathedral of Maringa which is 407ft and looks like a giant white cone. St. Patrick's Cathedral in Melbourne is 344ft and is the tallest in Australia. The tallest church in Asia at 285ft is the INC Central Temple in the Philippines. Rounding out the continental competition at a mere 49ft tall is Trinity Church on King George Island, Antarctica.

Cathedral of Maringa. *Mariordo (Mario Roberto Durán Ortiz) [CC BY-SA 3.0 (https://creativecommons.org/licenses/by-sa/3.0)]*

(opposite page) Ulm Minster. *Tilman2007 [CC BY-SA 3.0 (https://creativecommons.org/licenses/by-sa/3.0)]*

Monk Terms

The word monk comes from the Greek word *monos* meaning solitary. Anthony (251-356) often considered the first monk left all of his wealth and sought solitude in the desert of Egypt. The Greek word for desert is *eremos* from which we get the word hermit. It is also the word used in the gospels to describe the desolate places where Jesus went to pray

Saint Anthony, mosaic from Fethiye Museum. *Dosseman [CC BY-SA 4.0 (https://creativecommons.org/licenses/by-sa/4.0)]*

(ex. Matthew 14:13). After a few years of solitude others sought to imitate Anthony and built a community near the old monk. At first Anthony ignored them, but eventually he decided to instruct them. This laid the groundwork for monastic communities that lived in isolation. Around the 12th century the habit of monks living in isolated communities created an unintended consequence that emerged in several places at same time. The spiritual and physical needs of people in cities had been mostly ignored. Agile groups who followed similar monastic vows but freely worked outside of monasteries formed under men like Francis of Assisi (1182-1226) in present day Italy and Dominic of Osma (1170-1221) in present day Spain. These groups referred to themselves as brothers, in Latin *frater* and in Middle English *friar*. They are sometimes known as *mendicants* from the Latin word for beggar because of their reliance on the charity of others.

Hell, USA

There are plenty of biblical places that sound pleasant and are well suited to use when naming a place. One biblical place that isn't so pleasant surprisingly shows up quite often. Dryhill, Kentucky sounds like a nice enough place which is why it was chosen as the official name of a place that has long been known as Hell For Certain, Kentucky. In North Carolina there is a town named after a nearby swamp. Both town and swamp are known as Half Hell. If you want more than half, take a 15-minute drive from Ann Arbor and you'll be in Hell, Michigan. And yes it does freeze over several times a year. Ohio is home to two separate places about an hour apart that at different times have both been known as Hell Town. Gehenna is another biblical term for hell. It is a valley outside Jerusalem that you might have heard was used as a burning garbage dump and place to dispose of bodies. That's probably a made-up story dating to the 1200s, but Gehenna was a real place where child sacrifices to the false gods Molech and Baal occurred, specifically at a site known as Tophet. There is a Gahanna, Ohio (probably coincidental) and 8 separate places in Massachusetts named Tophet.

Sign from Hell, Michigan. *Sswonk [CC BY-SA 3.0 (https://creativecommons.org/licenses/by-sa/3.0)]*

Biddenden Maids

The Biddenden Maids were a pair of conjoined twins in Kent, England who upon their death left about 20 acres of land to the local church to thereafter provide a dole of bread, cheese and beer to the poor every Easter. The facts surrounding the sisters are not well known. Some accounts date them to the 12th century while others claim they lived in the 16th century or perhaps never existed at all. What is known is that the dole has been given since at least 1605, that a charity has existed since 1656 and that the disbursement quickly became a rowdy affair. Or at least it was until the Archbishop of Canterbury took away the free beer in 1882. At some point the poor were also given hard flour biscuits known as Biddenden cakes with the image of two women standing side by side stamped on the front. It is likely the image contributed to the legend of conjoined twins. The first account of the twins being conjoined dates from 1770, and it wasn't 1808 that their names were first listed as Eliza and Mary Chulkhurst. The tradition of giving the dole to the poor and elderly on Easter continues today to this day.

(above) Mold of Biddenden cake circa 1750. *Public Domain.*

(right) Biddenden Cakes and newspaper clipping. *Wellcome Collection [CC BY 4.0 (https://creativecommons.org/licenses/by/4.0)]*

God's Property

There have been a few times that someone deeded land to God. Celestia, Pennsylvania was intended to be a religious commune of people waiting for the end times. By deeding their land to God, they wrongly thought they could avoid taxes. The founder's son had to cover the

God's Acre Healing Springs. *Kilodawg06 [CC BY-SA 4.0 (https://creativecommons.org/licenses/by-sa/4.0)]*

taxes God neglected to pay. A second encounter with the government backfired even more spectacularly for Celestia. When they successfully petitioned President Lincoln for a draft exemption, the community became flooded with draft dodgers and its founder had to abandon the site. A much happier story of deeding land to God comes from Blackville, South Carolina. God's Acre Healing Springs is a small plot of land that contains a simple artesian well with a reputation for miraculous healing since at least the Revolutionary War. In 1944, then owner Lute Boylston deeded the spring to God so that it would forever be free for all. The property is maintained by Barnwell County and is open 24 hours a day. The county has not tried to collect taxes from God.

Moon Bible

Astronaut Edgar Mitchell. *US National Archives and Records Administration [Public domain]*

The Apollo Prayer League led by NASA chaplain Rev. John Stout had a mission to take the first bible to the moon. They did so by using a new technology, microfilm, which enabled the entire King James Bible to fit on a 1.6 square inch sheet. The miniature bible was to be stowed voluntarily as part of an astronaut's personal preference kit which was limited to a just few cubic inches. In total three attempts were made. During Apollo 12 a single copy of the Bible was taken on board by astronaut Alan Bean, but it was mistakenly placed in the command module and never made it to the moon's surface. During the next mission, the ill-fated Apollo 13, there were 512 bibles placed onboard which never made it to the moon. Finally, Apollo 14 with astronaut Edgar Mitchell was successful. Once again 512 bibles were onboard with 100 taken in the lunar module that went to the moon's surface. Once back on earth the 100 lunar bibles were given serial numbers by Stout and many were gifted to supporters of the Apollo Prayer League. One is on permanent display at the Museum of the Bible.

Black Church, White Pastor

Predominately black churches and denominations have historically had black pastors. But not always. The first denomination formed by black people in America was the African Methodist Episcopal Church in 1794 with the founding of Bethel AME in Philadelphia. From 1854-1863, Rev. George Nolley, a white man, served as the pastor of Third Street Bethel AME in Richmond, Virginia. In 1866, Rev. James Sisson joined the denomination serving in Virginia,

Bethel African Methodist Episcopal Church (second building circa 1829). *Library Company of Philadelphia [No restrictions]*

Georgia, and the Indian Territories (present day Oklahoma). Sisson worked to build churches among the estimated ten thousand blacks living among the tribes including many who were slaves under Indian masters. The most curious example is Rev. Louis Fenwick. In 1903, Fenwick was pastor of St. Mark's AME in Milwaukee. His house was allegedly robbed and during the trial Fenwick was called to testify. While on the witness stand, he was forced to reveal that he was in fact a white man. Unlike Nolley and Sisson, Fenwick had hidden his ethnicity, and the subsequent revelation shocked the city and split the congregation. Contemporary examples of nonblack pastors are more numerous, but one noteworthy pastor is the Rev. Sam Mann. He who grew up in rural Alabama during the civil rights movement and marched with Martin Luther King, Jr. Mann served for 40 years as the pastor at St. Mark Union Church in Kanasas City, Missouri.

Early American Converts

The first Christian converts in North America were likely converted by Spanish Catholic priests who began arriving in 1526. Though there is no record of the first individual conversion, some estimate as many as a million converts from Florida and through Mexico as far as California. The first confirmed individual conversion by English Christians was a member of the Croatan tribe (in present day North Carolina) named Manteo. He is believed to have been converted to Anglican Christianity around 1584 by Sir Walter Raleigh. In Alaska, the first Russian Orthodox monks settled on Kodiak Island in 1794 and set about converting the natives. In Hawaii, the first Christian is thought to be Henri Opukahaia (1792-1818) who at ten years old lost his parents and subsequently traveled aboard a merchant ship to Connecticut where he lived with ministers and was converted to Christianity. He died of typhoid fever before he could return as a missionary to Hawaii, but his zeal inspired others to go.

The 13. of August (1587), our Sauage Manteo, by the commandement of Sir Walter Ralegh, was christened in Roanoak, and called Lord thereof, and of Dasamongueponke, in reward of his faithfull seruice." The christening of Manteo is the first recorded admission of a North American Indian to the Church of England.

Sign commemorating Manteo. *Sarah Stierch [CC BY 4.0 (https://creativecommons.org/licenses/by/4.0)]*

(previous page) Kodiak Island, 1851. *Public Domain.*

Ice Holes

Epiphany Sunday according to Eastern Orthodox Christians marks the day that Jesus was baptized by John in the Jordan River. In Russia, Orthodox Christians have participated since at least 1525 in a celebration known as the Great Blessing of the Waters. During the ritual a priest would dip a cross in the water to commemorate the baptism of Jesus. The water would then become holy and was used to bless others. In modern times, Russians celebrate by immersing themselves in the water after the blessing. It is believed that the water has power to heal and forgive sin. Epiphany Sunday occurs in early January. For most parts of Russia this means that it is very cold and that the lakes are frozen. Cross shaped ice holes with temporary shelters called "iordans" are made for the ceremony. Russian President Vladimir Putin is a regular participant at Lake Seliger where the temperature is around -7C. In the vast region of Siberia temperatures during the evening ceremonies can range from -7C at the comparatively warm coastal areas to -50C in Yakutsk, the coldest city in the world. For reference, the naked human body will freeze to death in about a minute at -50C.

Man emerging from an ice hole. *RIA Novosti archive, image #179104 / Valery Titievsky / CC-BY-SA 3.0 [CC BY-SA 3.0 (https://creativecommons.org/licenses/by-sa/3.0)]*

Gretna Green

When you think of classic symbols for marriage you probably don't picture a blacksmith's anvil. But every year thousands of people in one Scottish town get married over an anvil in a tradition that dates back hundreds of years. In 1754 an English law was passed that allowed parents to veto the marriage of a child under 21 years old. However, the law was only applicable in England and Wales. Couples took advantage of the loophole and made their way to neighboring Scotland to wed. In 1770 a new road made the tiny village of Gretna Green, Scotland the closest place to wed. The most convenient place was the center of town which happened to be a blacksmith shop. Scottish law at the time allowed for almost anyone to officiate the ceremony, including blacksmiths. The enterprising smiths became known as "anvil priests" and would perform the ceremony for a nominal fee. One especially enterprising anvil priest named Richard Rennison took over the Old Blacksmith Shop in 1927 and was able to perform 5,147 weddings until the law temporarily banned the practice in 1940. Today over a million tourists visit Gretna Green each year and about 2000 couples get married.

Old Blacksmith Shop, 1930. *Willem van de Poll, Public Domain.*

(previous page) Postcard from 1911. *Public Domain.*

Cowboy Surfer Church

There are a few themed churches in America. Cowboy Church is one of the more popular examples. The first cowboy church was started by professional rodeo clown Glenn Smith in 1972 who wanted a place that rodeo workers would feel comfortable attending. Today there are an estimated 5000 cowboy churches doing church in a uniquely cowboy style. They are known for preaching simple messages with western style worship in nontraditional settings. Cowboy churches also don't do things that might make outsiders feel uncomfortable. For example, instead of taking up an offering, a boot is often set out by the entrance for anyone who wants to give a donation. Another popular themed church is surfer church with organizations like Christian Surfers that aim to minister to surfers. In 2002 they launched the first edition of the Surfer's Bible, an NLT translation with surfer testimonies and other surf-themed content. Other organizations like the Surf Church Collective exist to support surfer-friendly churches. There are dozens of surfer churches and surfer friendly churches in communities from coast to coast.

Humphrey Gainsborough, Inventor

Humphrey Gainsborough (1718-1776) was a pastor at the Independent Chapel in Henley-on-Thames, England. He was also a skilled engineer and inventor. He built a bridge that is still in use today and designed locks along the nearby river. He is credited with several inventions including a new kind of plough, a fireproof strongbox, and a water wheel called a tide-mill that could spin both ways to generate power. He is thought to have been the first to make significant improvements to the steam engine, but unfortunately was not the first to patent the design that made others rich. Gainsborough is also the inventor of the lesser known self-

Portrait of Humphrey Gainsborough painted by his brother Thomas Gainsborough, circa 1770. *Public Domain.*

ventilating fish-wagon. Probably his most enduring invention is a device common to many homes today, the door chain. Gainsborough created the security feature to allow the door to be partially opened. You can still see the original on his house beside the church where served.

Christian Endeavor

Most churches have a youth ministry and take for granted that you should minister to youth differently than you would to adults. But that hasn't always been the case. The first person credited with developing a youth ministry was Francis Edward Clark (1851-1927), a minister at Williston Congregational Church in Portland, Maine. He wanted to reach the young people (aged 13-30) in his church and believed that they could contribute immediately to the vitality of the church. At the time this was a radical idea. Youth were either part of the entire congregation or grouped with the young children. Separating out the youth was seen by naysayers as creating a church within a church. Unperturbed, Clark created a youth-only prayer meeting that eventually became the Williston Young People's Society for Christian Endeavor. Christian Endeavor, as it came to be known quickly spread beyond Clark's church and grew from 57 youths at the first meeting in 1885 to 2.5 million by 1895. Eventually the interdenominational ministry was imitated by denominations forming their own groups. At the same time Christian Endeavor saw a need to further specialize by creating three separate ministries by age range: 20-30s, teens, and children under 13. Once again these ideas began to take hold inside other churches giving rise to what we expect today.

Gathering of Christian Endeavor, 1921. *Bain News Service, publisher. Public domain.*

(previous page) Francis Edward Clark, wearing CE (Christian Endeavor) lapel pin. *Public Domain.*

Made in United States
Orlando, FL
25 April 2022

17166969R00081